Human Rights and Counter-terrorism in America's Asia Policy

Rosemary Foot

ADELPHI PAPER 363

9333689

Oxford University Press, Great Clarendon Street, Oxford OX2 6DP
Oxford New York

Athens Auckland Bangkok Bombay Calcutta Cape Town
Dar es Salaam Delhi Florence Hong Kong Istanbul Karachi
Kuala Lumpur Madras Madrid Melbourne Mexico City Nairobi
Paris Taipei Tokyo Toronto
and associated companies in Ibadan

Oxford is a trade mark of Oxford University Press

Published in the United States
by Oxford University Press Inc., New York

© The International Institute for Strategic Studies 2004

First published February 2004 by **Oxford University Press** for
The International Institute for Strategic Studies
Arundel House, 13–15 Arundel Street, Temple Place, London WC2R 3DX
www.iiss.org

Director John Chipman
Editor Tim Huxley
Design Manager Simon Nevitt

British Library Cataloguing in Publication Data
Data available

Library of Congress Cataloguing in Publication Data

ISBN 0-19-855002-2
ISSN 0567-932X

Contents

Introduction

One week after the terrorist attacks on US territory on 11 September 2001, US National Security Advisor Condoleezza Rice declared that: 'Civil liberties matter to this President very much, and our values matter to us abroad. We are not going to stop talking about the things that matter to us, human rights, [and] religious freedom ... We're going to continue to press these things; we would not be America if we did not'.[1] On many other occasions since 11 September, administration officials, including US President George W. Bush himself, have argued that when governments respect both the rule of law and human rights they contribute to a world where terrorism cannot thrive. For this reason, as well as the US commitment to the promotion of its values, the US claims that it will not relax its vigilance when it comes to the advancement of human rights.

Many other features of American society beyond its self-image bolster this Bush administration claim that it cannot put its externally directed human-rights policy aside. The numbers of non-governmental human-rights organisations, many of which have headquarters in either New York City or Washington DC, have dramatically increased over the years and they stand ready to expose and lobby against neglect of human-rights abuses. The level of US bureaucratic resources devoted to human-rights protection has also steadily expanded, as has the number of legislative commitments. Alongside the growth in the size of the US Department of State's Bureau of Democracy, Human Rights, and Labor (DRL), other parts of the federal government, such as the United States Agency for

International Development (USAID), have introduced human-rights components into their assistance programmes. As the concept of security has widened in meaning for much of the academic community – to embrace ideas that link human rights with human security, for example – these new understandings have appeared in a number of US governmental statements, as well as in actual policy.

Yet, it is also undeniable that, since 11 September, there are many examples that can be drawn upon to suggest that the US has compromised its stance in the sphere of human-rights promotion, as it searches for military bases, intelligence cooperation and political support in the struggle against terrorism. The US has moved closer to governments with poor human-rights records which it once shunned, has reversed or modified policies that were introduced in order to signal displeasure with a country's human-rights record, and has downgraded attention to human-rights conditions in some other nations. US national security officials have also been reported as using techniques outlawed under the 1984 Convention Against Torture and Other Cruel, Inhuman or Degrading Treatment or Punishment, which the US signed in 1994, in their interrogation of al-Qaeda suspects. US authorities have returned or sent a number of prisoners for further interrogation to countries where there are strong grounds to suspect that they will suffer torture.[2] Moreover, these compromises have run in parallel with a serious curtailment of fundamental civil liberties at home, including the detention of an estimated 5,000 or more non-US citizens on alleged but unproven terrorist grounds. These trends have undermined the international authority of the US stance in this issue area and imply that there has been a trade-off between the imperatives of security in the 'age of terror' and human-rights protection.[3]

This paper seeks to investigate how the two dimensions of national security and human rights are reflected in US policy towards a number of countries in Asia, which Washington views as valuable to the ongoing anti-terrorist campaign. Asia is important in this regard because, according to US estimates, in 2000 it accounted for 75% of the world's incidence of terrorist casualties. Others have described it as a region that is 'wracked by terrorist, insurgent, and separatist violence in a manner unmatched elsewhere in the world'. Much of this spread of terrorist activity has been linked to the war in Afghanistan in the 1980s, which drew Muslim fighters from all around the world, and where a large quantity of US-supplied weaponry found its way onto the black market, 'spreading illicit arms and militancy from Egypt to the Philippines'.[4] Notably, too, there are relatively few states in this region with good records in protecting human rights, and a number that had been the subject of US concern in this respect for several years.

After the 11 September attacks, the Bush administration came to designate certain states in Asia as front line, or as part of a second front in the struggle against terrorism. Some might be thought of as being in a third category, providing important intelligence and political support. These rankings set in train a re-evaluation and some reordering of priorities in relation to several of America's bilateral relationships. To determine the extent to which such a reordering has occurred, this analysis will concentrate on the front-line states of Pakistan and Uzbekistan, the second-front states of Indonesia and Malaysia, and one third-front country, China.

The significance of this investigation rests on an appreciation of the damage that can be done to the international human-rights regime when the US seriously compromises its previously highly visible, if blemished, role in promoting an external human-rights policy through bilateral and multilateral mechanisms, and drops its standards inside the US itself. This inquiry could, of course, be undertaken in respect of other democratic states, but a sole focus on the US can be justified as an important initial step. As the hegemonic state in the global system, the US has manifold resources at its disposal if it decides to give priority to the protection of human rights, including an extensive military- and economic-assistance programme, comprehensive foreign relations, and significant voting power within international financial institutions (IFIs). Its domestic and external policy positions in this issue area are closely monitored by other nations and societies, influencing these nations' behaviour for good or ill. When the US falters, the human-rights regime experiences a serious weakening.

The study's importance is also related to the contribution that it might make to understanding how US officials attempt to order their priorities in the fields of security and human rights, or whether they have found it necessary or appropriate to accord priority to one over the other at all. How has the US formulated policies designed to contribute to the anti-terrorist struggle towards states that, prior to 11 September 2001, would have been condemned for abusing the human rights of their populations?

The main conclusion of this paper is a qualified one. In general, it finds that, while it is inaccurate to assume that the human-rights issue no longer imposes any constraints on US policy towards these five governments, attention to that aspect of policy has indeed been compromised since 11 September. Moreover, all of these states have opportunistically exploited the room for manoeuvre offered by changes in US domestic and foreign policy. However, the degree of US compromise has not depended solely on the centrality of a particular state in the struggle against terrorism. This causal claim has to be combined with a domestic-level explanation: if there is strong domestic concern about the poverty of a country's human-rights record, then, even if that state is central to anti-terrorist operations, rhetorical attention to human-rights conditions within the country remain prominent. Human-rights concerns thus retain some place, if generally at the discursive level, in US foreign policy for political, normative and institutional reasons.

Chapter 1

US Foreign- and Domestic-policy Realignments After 11 September

The US response to the events of 11 September has been notable for its comprehensiveness. Budgetary, bureaucratic and legislative changes, each with far-reaching ramifications, have been made with remarkable speed. The military budget, in particular, has risen substantially. Set at $296.2 billion for Fiscal Year (FY) 2001, the request for FY03 was for $396.8bn – the largest annual increase since US President Ronald Reagan entered office in 1981 – with the expectation that it will grow to $469.8bn by FY07.[1] Whereas in 2000, the US spent as much on its military as the next eight countries combined, in 2001, that had broadened to the next 15, and, in 2002, to the next 20.[2] Within six weeks of 11 September, the US Congress had passed a USA Patriot Act that gave sweeping new powers to various US governmental agencies in the areas of surveillance, intelligence and detention. The congressional bill, passed in November 2002, that created a Department of Homeland Security, has brought together some 170,000 US employees from 22 federal agencies, representing most of the main elements of domestic security.[3]

Foreign policy

The US decision to take the fight against al-Qaeda to Afghanistan and to overthrow the Taliban regime led it to forge new alignments in Central Asia, most notably with Pakistan and states such as Kyrgyzstan and Uzbekistan. These countries provided much vital assistance for that military campaign and were quickly rewarded with economic aid – directly or via the IFIs – and military cooperation.

Whereas before 11 September, the Department of Defense had no military bases in Central Asia, some six months later it had access to over a dozen. The requirements of intelligence sharing, assistance with freezing terrorist assets, and the need for coordinated policing resulted in a deepening of exchanges with many other governments in Asia, including China, Indonesia, Malaysia and the Philippines.

Singapore also proved to be an important source of intelligence on active trans-regional terrorist groupings – actually foiling a plot in December 2001 to launch attacks on US and other Western targets. In addition, it provided practical assistance in facilitating air-to-air refuelling and offered port facilities to US carrier battle groups as American forces took on the Taliban and al-Qaeda.

Well beyond these practical requirements of the counter-terrorist struggle, the US has found support from such states, especially those with large Muslim populations, potentially useful in trying to project this war as one not against Islam but solely against terrorism. Moreover, China and Malaysia are also important for political and institutional reasons. China, as a permanent member of the United Nations (UN) Security Council, voted in favour of Resolution 1368 under Chapter VII of the UN Charter, which legitimated the US attack on Afghanistan – the first time that Beijing had voted in favour of the potential international use of force. China also happened to be hosting (in Shanghai) the October 2001 Asia-Pacific Economic Cooperation (APEC) Summit, an occasion that allowed support to be voiced for the US in its hour of need. For several months after 11 September, Malaysia was projected in the US as a successful, moderate Muslim nation that has been a beacon of stability in Southeast Asia. Knowing that Malaysia would be the incoming head of the countries that make up the Organisation of the Islamic Conference (OIC), Washington became keener still to improve relations with Kuala Lumpur.

A further consequence of the globalised threat of terrorism has been the dispatch around the world of many thousands of US troops, mostly members of the Special Forces. In the Philippines, for example, more than 1,000 US military troops were deployed in early 2002 to provide support for search-and-destroy operations directed against the Abu Sayyaf Group. Manila has also been the recipient of some $356 million in US security-related assistance for 2003 and 2004, and, in November 2002, it signed a Mutual Logistics Support Agreement with Washington allowing the US enhanced access to air and naval bases in the country. This is an unanticipated turnaround from its decision of the early 1990s not to renew the US basing agreements at Clark and Subic Bay. These two former bases are now being used as transit points for US matériel and personnel involved in counter-terrorist operations in the Philippines.[4]

The Bush administration has also offered to provide training in the US in counter-terrorism techniques. Members of the military of Indonesia, among other countries, have been offered counter-terrorism fellowships. In July 2002, Washington also requested Malaysia's help in establishing a regional counter-terrorism centre in Kuala Lumpur.

Such developments have drawn the US into closer contact and more cooperative relations with states that, in the past, had often been subject to official US criticism on account of their human-rights records. For instance, the seizure of power in October 1999 by General Pervez Musharraf of Pakistan from an elected civilian leadership led to the final cutting off of all US aid, already severely curtailed following Pakistan's nuclear tests in 1998. Shortly after Pakistan had agreed in September 2001 to offer US armed forces an air corridor into Afghanistan, most of those sanctions were suspended and Washington helped to assemble International Monetary Fund (IMF) and World Bank loans and to restructure Islamabad's bilateral debt. As these examples show, sometimes there are material reasons for closer alignment between the US and Asian states – the military, political and intelligence support that these nations have offered. In other cases, there are additional, important, symbolic reasons for seeking their support.

Domestic legislative changes and their effects on civil liberties in the US

Within one week of the 11 September attacks, US Attorney General John Ashcroft brought the USA Patriot Act before the US Congress. The act amends 15 different federal statutes and awards sweeping new powers to law-enforcement and intelligence agencies. Areas of law affected include those relating to immigration, surveillance and intelligence sharing. Although Congress ultimately took six weeks to pass this bill into law (on 26 October 2001), rather than the three days that Ashcroft asserted it would require, little time was available for due deliberation of its provisions or for much in the way of public hearings.[5]

The consequences that have flowed from the enactment of some elements of the USA Patriot Act, or from new interpretations of earlier legislation, have been disturbing. Some 1,200 non-citizens, mostly Muslim men, were detained in the US immediately after the 2001 terrorist strikes, with estimates of above 5,000 in US custody as of May 2003.[6] As the Department of Justice's Office of the Inspector General concluded in a report released on 2 June 2003, these men were held in harsh confinement, often without access to lawyers, and denied all chance of bail. Some at a facility in Brooklyn, New York, were held in highly restricted 23-hour 'lockdown' conditions, only being allowed to move outside of their cells once they had been handcuffed or strapped with leg irons and heavy chains. Seven hundred and sixty two were found to be illegal immigrants, and most were eventually deported, but none were charged as terrorists.[7]

In November 2001, Bush authorised the use of special military commissions to try non-citizens accused of supporting or engaging in terrorist activity. Although the worst of the abrogations of due process were corrected in new regulations issued in March 2002, the special military tribunals nevertheless reinforced the perception that it had become acceptable for a number of US due-process safeguards to be set aside. In Bush's view, it was simply 'not practicable' to try terrorists under the 'principles of law and the rules of evidence' to which Americans had become accustomed within their own criminal-justice system.[8]

The Department of Justice also drew on earlier legislation to water down the rules of evidence required to prove intent to engage in or to further terrorism. The Antiterrorism and Effective Death Penalty Act, passed in 1996, and rarely employed before 11 September 2001, has made it a criminal offence to provide material support to any group that has been designated as 'terrorist', whatever the intention behind that support. Two US citizens described by Bush as 'enemy combatants' have been held for two years without charges being filed; only in December 2003 is one being given access to counsel – according to the Department of Defense 'as a matter of discretion' and not a requirement in law. The US government has claimed that its actions are consistent with the laws of war, but that designation of 'enemy combatant' has been challenged in the US courts and by non-governmental human-rights organisations.[9]

According to former Assistant Secretary of State for DRL, the international lawyer and scholar Harold Hongju Koh, legislation of this kind serves to reject three principles by which the US has balanced national security and civil liberties since the Second World War:

1. the separation of the domestic and foreign realms in order to prevent the government from spying on Americans and to protect rights guaranteed under the US Constitution;
2. the granting of civil rights to lawfully admitted 'aliens', comparable to those of other citizens, thus ruling out the notion that 'foreign born Americans or immigrants have only second class rights'; and
3. the acknowledgement of the executive branch's lead on national security issues, while insisting that 'its actions be subject to congressional oversight and judicial review'.[10]

Prisoners of the war in Afghanistan

Another major area of controversy concerns the 625 or so prisoners picked up as a result of the fighting in Afghanistan and since held at the US naval base at Guantanamo Bay, Cuba. They have not been accorded prisoner-of-war status, although the White House eventually announced that the principles of the third Geneva Convention would be applied to them. None has been charged. And while about 35 were released in March and May 2003 (including a juvenile), they were replaced by around two dozen shortly thereafter.[11] Controversy surrounding their status under international law has been seriously compounded by photographs distributed around the world of these prisoners in orange overalls crouching before US marine commanders, blindfolded and shackled.[12]

Allegations made in December 2002 that prisoners held at the US-occupied Bagram air base in Afghanistan have been tortured while in US custody, or as a result of being sent to third countries for further interrogation where torture is routinely practiced, have lent support to the argument that the Bush administration regards 11 September as a major watershed in its attitude towards adherence to human-rights norms. According to a *Washington Post* article: 'national security officials interviewed for this article defended the use of violence against captives as just and necessary. They expressed confidence that the American public would back their view'. As one official supervising the capture and transfer of alleged terrorists told a *Washington Post* reporter: 'If you don't violate someone's human rights some of the time, you probably aren't doing your job'.[13] Finally, over three months after the publication of that article, the General Counsel of the Department of Defense, William J. Haynes, wrote to the Executive Director of Human Rights Watch, Kenneth Roth, underlining that the US government 'condemns and prohibits torture' and, if enemy combatants are detained in other countries on behalf of the US, 'appropriate assurances that such enemy combatants are not tortured' are sought. Human Rights Watch noted that the letter did not 'acknowledge that the United States has a legal obligation to refrain from cruel, inhuman or degrading treatment' and ignored the reports regarding the use of 'stress and duress' techniques.[14]

Chapter 2

The Place of Human Rights in US Foreign Policy

These developments appear to have constrained the prospects for a human-rights dimension to US foreign policy. They offer political cover, too, for abusive governments to take advantage and crackdown on those individuals and groups that they would like to silence for reasons other than their potential links with terrorism. Asian governments have claimed parallels between internal security acts in their own countries and the USA Patriot Act, have passed new or expanded legislation that has given police new powers of arrest and detention, and have taken note of the possible US use of torture against prisoners held incommunicado in various overseas facilities. When Mary Robinson signed off as United Nations High Commissioner for Human Rights in September 2002, she recorded her apprehensiveness about the impact of 11 September on human rights. At a meeting in Geneva, Switzerland, she noted that many of the special rapporteurs and chairs of various treaty bodies had warned of the 'erosion of civil liberties' around the world in the 'guise of combating terrorism'.

Robinson, however, also stated what has become a noted trend since the 1980s: that human rights had become 'the dominant moral vocabulary in foreign affairs'.[1] As Robinson put it, human rights are 'now firmly on the agenda of the international community'. She continued: 'If one thinks back twenty years to arguments about whether human rights were universal, whether they could be made operational, whether they have a serious place in the conduct of international relations, one would have to conclude that human rights have indeed come a long way ... There is much greater recognition now of the centrality of human rights and the immense benefits a rights-based approach brings'.[2] This is a view that has also been expressed in the academic literature on the subject. As Jack Donnelly wrote in 1998: 'In contrast to the 1970s and early 1980s, when debate often focused on whether human rights should be an active foreign policy concern, today the question is usually which rights to emphasize in which particular cases'.[3]

It is undeniable, furthermore, that the human-rights idea has become embedded in US legislation, in the country's self-image, and within its bureaucracy. For many years, the US government has played a major, if inconsistent, role in maintaining a focus on the extent of human-rights protections in other countries, and in the last three decades has argued that this is a legitimate area of international concern.[4] The US Congress took a lead and introduced legislation in the 1970s that sought to deny US assistance to those nations that engaged in gross human-rights violations. It would be unrealistic to assume that 30 years of action in this issue area would now impose no constraints on the operation of US foreign policy worldwide.

The US commitment to an external human-rights policy

The US commitment to promoting human rights grew out of the pressures associated with the US civil-rights movement, the character and outcome of the Vietnam War, and the amoral aspects of the behaviour of the administration of US President Richard Nixon. Congressional reaction to many of the unsavoury elements of US foreign policy at a time of poor relations between the executive and legislative branches prompted a change.[5] Basically, Congress introduced a variety of legislative instruments that sought to deny economic and military aid – whether administered bilaterally or via the IFIs – to any government that engaged in gross violations of internationally recognised human rights. It led US President Jimmy Carter to establish a special interagency group, known as the Christopher Group (after Warren Christopher), to help implement these congressional requirements. Although this policy was subject to political bias, it had the overall effect of raising awareness of human-rights conditions abroad, because it required investigation of the human-rights record of many countries before decisions could be reached. In addition, Congress mandated the Department of State to file reports on the human-rights practices of all nations receiving security assistance, and eventually on all countries that were members of the UN.

The Carter administration set about restructuring the Department of State as a result, upgrading the post of human-rights coordinator to the level of assistant secretary. Between 1977 and 1979, the number of staff associated with what was then called the Bureau of Human Rights and Humanitarian Affairs rose from two to 29 (it now stands at over 90). Each regional bureau created a full-time post of human-rights officer to work directly with the Human Rights Bureau. The Department of State's obligation to produce country reports on human-rights conditions within nations that were UN members had the effect of altering the practices and norms within the Department of State. Accurate and unbiased human-rights reporting became 'an intrinsically important goal for many key actors'.[6] The public debate that ensued once the reports were submitted to Congress helped to increase, over time, their consistency, accuracy and comprehensiveness. When some non-governmental organisations (NGOs) began to publish their critiques of the reports, these were sent to US embassies for use in constructing reports the following year. Embassies recognised that, in order to comply with the congressional legislation and to satisfy or shield from criticism high-level officials within the Department of State, they would have to obtain better quality information. This led to the establishment of links with local human-rights organisations, or with political activists, potentially deepening US understanding of the countries in question. Overall, levels of awareness about, and resources devoted to, human-rights matters increased within the US Congress, the Department of State, and the NGOs.

In the past few decades, human-rights NGOs – whether operating trans-nationally or locally – have grown substantially in number. As mentioned above, many of these have offices or headquarters in the US, especially in New York City and Washington DC, because of the lobbying opportunities this affords (the IMF, the UN and the World Bank to name but a few institutions are located in these two cities). Between 1950 and 1993, the number of international groups working primarily on human rights increased fivefold, with a doubling between 1983 and 1993.[7] The UN and individual governments have become highly dependent on the information that

NGOs provide. NGOs have become major contributors to policy developments in the human-rights field: drafting resolutions in collaboration with UN officials; offering their findings as the basis for questioning states that submit reports to treaty bodies or that engage in 'bilateral dialogue' on the issue with the US government; and providing legal expertise in the formulation of new human-rights-related conventions. There is an interdependence between the NGOs and government officials that has legitimised the former's role in policymaking. This is especially so in the US, where the openness of government affords regular access and opportunities for the NGO to present its case and policy prescriptions.

Moreover, there have been moves within the US government to 'subcontract' to the NGO elements of policy that have a bearing on human-rights protections in various countries – for example: the running of legal training programmes for the judiciary, police or military in target countries; help with setting up legal aid centres; developing university-level courses in human rights; and the monitoring of elections. Such subcontracting has its particular attractions at a time when the US government might not want directly to pressure an important anti-terrorist ally in the human-rights area because of a desire to promote other forms of cooperation. As the President of the National Endowment for Democracy (NED), Carl Gershman, noted when testifying before Congress, it was possible for the short-term goal of protecting the security of US citizens and the longer-term goal of promoting democracy 'to collide'. Offering the example of a US ambassador in a non-democratic Middle Eastern country who was seeking to gain that government's permission to allow the stationing of US troops in the country in order to aid the fight against terrorists, Gershman said: 'In the midst of such a delicate situation, can we realistically ask the Embassy to be responsible for providing assistance to the very kinds of voices that the host government perceives as its opposition?' The answer to that rhetorical question might be obvious, but he went on to remind Congress that the US would pay a price 'down the road' if it did not reach out to those opposition figures who represented democratic voices in the country in question. Gershman suggested handing the problem over to the NED, because for that body 'such choices do not have to be made, since our sole mission is the promotion of democracy. Indeed, it was precisely this scenario that the founders of NED had in mind when they structured it as a non-governmental institution'.[8]

Some sections of the US media have also become alert to the human-rights implications of US foreign policies. They regularly cover NGO press releases and elicit information from these organisations. Journalists often ask US officials directly whether human-rights matters have been touched on during a meeting with a particular leader, or how a US official intends to maintain attention to the human-rights record of an abusive government, given the requirements of cooperation in the struggle against terrorism. They call on NGOs to remind them of the official US language used and past commitments made with respect to states that violate human rights.

Of course, each US administration has been selective about which countries' human-rights records receive attention, and which of the rights covered in the two core international human-rights covenants – the 1966 International Covenant on Civil and Political Rights (ICCPR) and the 1966 International Covenant on Economic, Social and Cultural Rights (ICESCR) – should be given priority. During the Carter era, for example, China was absent as a country of concern. However, his administration was also notable for its willingness to sign the ICCPR and the ICESCR, and for its focus on abuse in Latin America as well as in the Soviet bloc. Reagan tended to focus on the 'evil empire' – the former Soviet Union and its Eastern European allies, together with Cuba – to the neglect of such countries as Chile, China, El Salvador and Guatemala.

Post-Cold War attention to human rights

In the 1990s, and with the ending of the Cold War, US presidents initially appeared to worry less about where to focus attention when it came to promoting human rights and, in general, human rights received greater prominence both domestically and externally. For example, the US government finally ratified the ICCPR in 1992, and in 1994 both the Convention Against Torture and Other Cruel, Inhuman or Degrading Treatment or Punishment and the Convention on the Elimination of All Forms of Racial Discrimination (it has still not ratified the ICESCR), making its own practices subject to international scrutiny.[9] Events such as the army's attack on peaceful demonstrators in China on 4 June 1989, or militia and military abuses in East Timor in the 1990s, served to force human-rights questions to the top of the US agenda in its dealings with Beijing and Jakarta, at least for a time. During the administration of US President Bill Clinton, matters of religious freedom began to mount as an issue of concern. In October 1998, Clinton signed into law the International Religious Freedom Act, which mandated both the establishment of an Office of International Religious Freedom within the Department of State as well as an independent, bipartisan US Commission on International Religious Freedom, and the production of an annual report modelled on the Department of State's *Country Reports on Human Rights Practices*. The US also participated – sometimes via the UN, sometimes via the North Atlantic Treaty Organisation (NATO), or as a member of 'coalitions of the willing' – in a number of interventions that had a strong humanitarian dimension to them. As Adam Roberts has noted, there were nine cases between 1991 and 1999 where the UN Security Council debated the 'question of whether or not external institutions should, on basically humanitarian grounds, organize or authorize military action within a state, whether with or without its consent'.[10]

Developments within USAID in the 1990s also reflected greater involvement in promoting democratic reform, including better protection of human rights.[11] In 1994, USAID established the Office of Transition Initiatives (OTI) with a mandate to support 'peaceful democratic change in countries of strategic importance and humanitarian concern to the United States'. Thus, it became active (using grantees such as the National Democratic Institute) in trying to strengthen legislative, media, and other civil-society capacities in countries undergoing a democratic transition. After the fall of President Suharto in 1998, Indonesia became a prime recipient of assistance under this particular mandate, with the OTI funding such activities as elections, the media, civil-society groupings, and the reform of civil–military relations in the country.

From 1990, USAID also worked with the US Department of Defense to establish programmes designed to strengthen civilian control over militaries in order to curb the intervention of the armed forces in the governmental policymaking process. This led the Pentagon to set up the Expanded International Military Education and Training Program (E-IMET), the purpose of which was 'to contribute to responsible defense resource management, foster greater respect for and understanding of the principle of civilian control of the military, contribute to cooperation between military and law enforcement personnel with respect to counternarcotics law enforcement efforts, and improve military justice systems and procedures in accordance with internationally recognized human rights'.[12]

Such programmes represented a wider acceptance in the post-Cold War era that the concept of security represented something more than the security of states, that international order depended on an individual's own sense of security, and that human-rights violations on an extensive scale served to undermine not only the security of individuals and groups, but also regional and global order.[13] That is why many of the interventions sanctioned by the UN came under Chapter VII. Human-rights abuses, especially by those branches of the security apparatus – the armed forces, police, paramilitary and intelligence organisations – that have instruments of coercion at their disposal, can lead to destabilising flows of refugees, or to the adoption of desperate counter-measures and a consequent increase in violence.[14]

The George W. Bush administration

This linkage has lived on in the neo-Reaganite Bush administration since 2001 and imbues a number of the speeches given by the president as well as by members of his administration. The notion of human security allows for connections to be made between realist and liberal rhetoric. Those described as 'neo-conservative' have accepted the idea of the 'democratic peace' (that democracies tend not to go to war against each other) and that other types of regime are, therefore, potential sources of threat, capable of disturbing world order. This thinking contributed to Bush's decision to describe Iraq, Iran and North Korea in his January 2002 State of the Union address as an 'axis of evil'.[15] Bush portrayed North Korea as a 'regime arming with missiles and weapons of mass destruction, while starving its citizens'. Rice advanced the argument a couple of days later, saying that North Korea is 'the world's number one merchant for ballistic missiles, open for business with anyone, no matter how malign the buyer's intentions'. On 5 February, Secretary of Defense Donald Rumsfeld added that North Korea had imprisoned nearly 200,000 people in detention camps.[16]

These kinds of interconnections affected the way in which the war against the Taliban came to be presented. From emphasising a 'retributive strike', Bush moved to highlighting 'the Taliban regime and its mistreatment of the Afghan civilian population … as the real evil', which had to be rooted out. Equating the Taliban and the terrorists who had attacked the US as one and the same, Bush, in November 2001, argued that these two forces promoted 'terror abroad and impose[d] a reign of terror on the Afghan people'. In the aforementioned State of the Union address, self-defence had clearly been dropped in favour of linking the struggle against terrorism with the protection of human rights. It was in this speech that Bush made clear what his administration meant by human rights: 'America will always stand firm for the non-negotiable demands of human dignity: the rule of law; limits on the power of the state; respect for women; private property; free speech; equal justice; and religious tolerance ... we have a greater objective than eliminating threats and containing resentment. We seek a just and peaceful world beyond the war on terror'.[17]

The opening paragraph of the September 2002 US National Security Strategy (NSS) continued the theme, claiming that, in this century, 'only nations that share a commitment to protecting basic human rights and guaranteeing political and economic freedom will be able to unleash the potential of their people and assure their future prosperity'. It went on to warn that terrorists would thrive where there was an absence of rule of law and a failure to protect human dignity. The NSS promised a 50% increase in US core development aid (the Millennium Challenge Account), which would be made available to those developing countries that agreed to 'fight corruption, respect basic human rights, embrace the rule of law, invest in health care and education, follow responsible economic policies, and enable entrepreneurship'.[18]

It has proven to be a relatively small step to move from this argument to the idea that preventive action might need to be taken to stop weak states or so-called rogue regimes forming or maintaining links with terrorist groupings. The Bush administration made this a key plank in its case for war against Iraqi President Saddam Hussein. The NSS promises that the US will 'help nations that need our assistance in combating terror. And America will hold to account nations that are compromised by terror ... And, as a matter of common sense and self-defense, America will act against such emerging threats before they are fully formed'.

For the Bush administration, therefore, human-rights concerns enter the policymaking environment for two main reasons. First as a result of the bureaucratic and legislative commitments made since the 1970s, which have steadily been deepened and expanded. And second, because of the administration's acceptance latterly of the idea that gross human-rights violations generally tend to be the mark of a weak state – one that might, wittingly or not, provide the base from which terrorist cells can operate, or be hospitable to the establishment of links with transnational terrorism, and one that is likely to be the source of instability beyond its own borders. In some respects, this is a dangerous confluence of the two areas of human rights and security, since Bush administration officials have come to associate them with the US use of preventive military force against the abusive government, with all of the moral dilemmas that this raises in its wake.[19] In addition, the struggle against terrorism and 'rogue states', as Michael Ignatieff has argued, is absorbing most if not all of America's 'available political and military resources'. The overthrow of such regimes could eventually result in human-rights improvements in the targeted nations, but this possible outcome has to be weighed against the vacuum that is left when intervention on humanitarian grounds has to be contemplated in the next case of Rwanda-style genocide.[20]

This finding of the continuing if newly selective attention to the human-rights idea, needs to be considered alongside the two main components of my earlier argument: first, that there has been a serious erosion of civil liberties in the US and a disregard of international law in its treatment of prisoners at Guantanamo Bay, which has led to a reduction in US international moral authority; and, second, that the US administration has found it necessary to move closer to many governments with poor human-rights records for material and symbolic reasons. At a minimum, it suggests that there is a struggle in the US to frame policy towards a variety of states in Asia – a struggle that will be investigated in the five case studies that follow.

Chapter 3

Pakistan and Uzbekistan: the Front-line States

Pakistan and Uzbekistan have been key front-line states in the struggle against terrorism, especially in the initial aftermath of 11 September and the decision to overthrow the Taliban regime and its al-Qaeda allies. Both countries have long borders with Afghanistan and have provided direct access to the country, as well as intimate knowledge of the Taliban. More negatively, they have proven to be fertile recruitment grounds for al-Qaeda and other Islamist movements. US coincidences of interest with these two countries have led to their projection as important allies, and, as a result, the forging of much closer material and political relationships.

Pakistan

Nowhere was this shift in the US policy stance after 11 September more evident than in the case of Pakistan. From the status virtually of a failing or rogue state – fragile, with a nuclear capacity, and under a military dictatorship – Pakistan's status has become that of vital partner, resulting in increases in US military and economic aid, and regular high-level contacts. These included a visit by the Pakistani president to Camp David, Maryland, in June 2003, making Musharraf the first South Asian leader ever to be invited to the US president's mountain retreat. In exchange, Pakistan has provided access to its air space and military bases, supplied intelligence on al-Qaeda, and helped to arrest some of its key operatives.

US–Pakistan relations before 11 September

US administrations had enjoyed good relations with Pakistan during the Cold War, welded together in the US case through its anti-Soviet containment policy and on Pakistan's side because of a desire for security assistance to counter its primary enemy, India. Bilateral relations were particularly strong in the 1950s, and again in the 1980s after the Soviet intervention in Afghanistan. In 1981, the Reagan administration offered Pakistan – then led by General Zia ul-Haq – a $3.2bn, five-year economic and military aid package, and the country became an important channel for supplying arms to the Afghan resistance. In 1986, the Reagan administration made available $4bn over six years, despite Zia's continuing domination of the civilian-led government that had come to power in 1985.[1]

However, Pakistan's nuclear ambitions, the Soviet departure from Afghanistan in January 1989, and the role of Pakistan's army in helping to remove elected civilian Prime Minister Benazir Bhutto from power in August 1990 finally led, in October 1990, to the implementation of severe US sanctions. All military aid and most economic assistance were cut off. Seventy-one F-16 fighters that Pakistan had ordered in 1989, 28 of which had been paid for, were not delivered. Left intact was food aid of about $5m, which continued in FY97 and FY98. Once Pakistan had carried out its six nuclear tests in May 1998 further sanctions were put in place, including restrictions on trade, and denial of support from the US Export-Import Bank, and from the IFIs. The military coup in Pakistan in October 1999, which ousted Prime Minister Nawaz Sharif, and brought Musharraf to power, appeared to be the final straw. Within a few days, Musharraf had announced the suspension of the constitution and parliament, and the formation of a six-member National Security Council beholden to him as chief executive. The US Department of State stopped all remaining economic assistance and called on the new leader to implement democratic rule in the country. During Clinton's tour of the subcontinent in March 2000, he spent five days in India, but only a few hours in Pakistan, where he urged the military to restore democracy, seek a peaceful resolution to the conflict in Kashmir, and cease its support for the Taliban.[2]

The new Bush administration continued to differentiate between India and Pakistan, drawing the former closer to it for strategic and ideological reasons, and pushing Pakistan into increasing international isolation.[3] As Sumit Ganguly has written, before 11 September, 'the administration of George W. Bush had nearly relegated Pakistan to the category of a "rogue state" because of its military dictatorship, its support for the Taliban regime ... its feckless involvement in the ethnoreligious insurgency in the Indian-controlled regions of Kashmir, and its habit of shopping for nuclear and ballistic missiles in China and North Korea'.[4] Evidence that the Pakistani government had provided North Korea with the designs for centrifuges to enrich uranium in exchange for those missiles only added to the potential catalogue of charges that could have been laid at Islamabad's door.[5]

The importance of Pakistan after 11 September

The attacks on Washington DC and New York City immediately forced a reappraisal of Pakistan's international role. With the US decision to attack al-Qaeda forces and their Taliban hosts, Pakistan could offer Washington a great deal, including access to its air space and military bases, logistical support, intelligence, and help with the identification of targets.[6] It also permitted the rounding-up of militants in Pakistan itself,[7] leading in March 2003, for example, to the arrest of Khaled Sheikh Mohammed, the alleged planner of the 11 September strikes.[8] In all, Pakistan's security forces apprehended some 500 suspected al-Qaeda operatives between autumn 2001 and March 2003.[9]

Musharraf's statements of support in the immediate aftermath of the terrorist attacks were of significance to a US administration trying to demonstrate that its war was not against Islamic states in general, but against particular forms of extremism. The Pakistani president affirmed to a congressional committee in February 2002 that he wanted Pakistan to be a 'liberal, tolerant and strong Islamic state'. Bush and US Secretary of State Colin Powell also chose to interpret Musharraf's speech of 12 January 2002, given in Urdu on Pakistani television, as a positive break with the past. In that speech, Musharraf pledged to turn his country into a moderate state that would neither tolerate extremism nor be a safe haven for terrorists operating across its borders.[10] Musharraf suggested that he could bring others in the Islamic world with him: announcing his support for the US campaign against the Taliban, he confirmed that the OIC had endorsed Pakistan's position.[11]

Undoubtedly, if Pakistan had refused to support the US, this would have threatened the survival of the regime. In this instance, 'Pakistan would have been targeted by the US-led international coalition for its support of the Taliban and linked, by association, with their al-Qaeda guests'.[12] Instead, these Pakistani pledges of support received their anticipated reward. On 22 September 2001, Bush, with congressional support, waived the economic sanctions that had been imposed on Pakistan after its nuclear tests, and authorised US officials to approve loans and lines of credit negotiated with the IMF and World Bank. On 30 October, the democracy sanctions introduced in the wake of the 1999 military coup were also lifted. By November, Bush announced some $1bn in overall assistance to cover such items as direct budgetary support, trade promotion, anti-terrorism assistance, and relief for Afghan refugees housed in the country.[13] Two months later, USAID restarted its operations, with a plan to spend $624.5m in FY02 and $250m in FY03, focusing its efforts on improving the public education system, supporting the agricultural sector, and extending healthcare.[14] In August 2002, Washington signed an agreement with Islamabad designed to reschedule and consolidate some $3bn in Pakistani debt, $2.3bn to become repayable over 38 years, and the rest repayable over 23 years.[15] The US also authorised military sales worth $400m,[16] although, importantly, it did not agree to reactivate the deal for the F-16s. Musharraf's visit to the US in June 2003 saw the signing of a trade and investment framework agreement, and a pledge – subject to congressional approval – to provide $3bn in aid over five years, around half of which would be military assistance.[17]

The Bush administration additionally offered political legitimacy to the Musharraf government. During the general's state visit to Washington DC in February 2002, Bush described him as 'a leader of great courage and vision', and at the Camp David gathering in June 2003 as 'no better partner in our fight [against] terror'. In late September 2002, a meeting of the US–Pakistan Defense Consultative Group took place, the first since the imposition of sanctions after the May 1998 nuclear tests.

In these circumstances, what kind of attention could be given to human rights in US policy towards Pakistan? To return to the central dilemma referred to earlier, is this not a clear case where the short-term goal of protecting US citizens and the longer-term objective of promoting democracy and human rights 'collide'?

The US and the promotion of human rights and democracy

Pakistanis have suffered greatly due to human-rights abuses over the years. Sectarian violence has been a huge problem, many women have been the subject of 'honour' killings by male members of their family, and have been sexually assaulted sometimes as a punishment for alleged transgressions – to name but a few areas that concern the domestic and transnational human-rights communities. In addition, constitutional safeguards have regularly been suspended, and human-rights activists have been killed or threatened.[18]

The US Department of State's human-rights reports on Pakistan have not shied away from detailing such abuses, even after 11 September, describing Pakistan's record generally as 'poor'. The 2002 report, for example, focused on the involvement of the police in extrajudicial killings, arbitrary arrest, trafficking in women and children, and the prevalence of honour killings.[19] The 2003 report noted a worsening of police involvement in extrajudicial killings. The *International Religious Freedom* report of 2002 designated Pakistan as one of 12 'countries of particular concern' under the International Religious Freedom Act.[20]

In other respects, however, there has been equivocation on the part of the Bush administration. In 2002, the Department of State released its second annual *Trafficking in Persons* report. Originally in the third and more serious tier of concern, Pakistan was moved to Tier 2 in 2002, despite the fact that, not until late August 2002, did it sign a legal protocol against trafficking and there had been little evidence of a reduction in the problem. Human-rights organisations have suggested that this improved status represented a reward for its front-line role in the fight against terrorism.[21]

In fact, relatively little – apart from in the Department of State's reports – has appeared about human rights per se in US official discussion of Pakistan after 11 September. Rather than focusing on rights, the US administration has given more attention to the issue of democracy – in particular, a return to civilian government and the holding of democratic elections. As noted earlier, in October 2001, Bush removed the democracy sanctions that had been imposed after the October 1999 coup. He issued another executive order in 2003 to continue to waive the sanctions first imposed in 1999. Some members of Congress expressed discomfort at this;[22] thus, in order to ease the political repercussions of those determinations, US officials have sought to supply evidence that Musharraf has been working towards the ending of military rule. In May 2000, the general had agreed to abide by a Pakistani Supreme Court ruling that national elections would be held no later than 90 days after 12 October 2002, the third anniversary of the coup. That promise proved to be important to US officials, as each clung to that intention as a way of trying to balance a relationship that appeared to be based predominantly on national security needs. During Powell's visit to Islamabad in October 2001, which was designed to cement that security relationship, he referred approvingly to Musharraf's 'commitment to return Pakistan to democracy', a commitment that would 'enhance his effort to deepen social reform, improve education, and improve the lives of his people'.[23] During Musharraf's visit to Washington DC in February 2002, Bush noted his pleasure at the decision to hold elections in October, and more particularly that Musharraf had 'articulated a vision of a Pakistan as a progressive, modern, and democratic society, determined and serious about seeking greater learning and greater prosperity for its citizens'.[24]

The problem was that, coincident with these statements, Musharraf was continuing to concentrate power in his own hands. At the end of April 2002, he held a national referendum designed to allow him to remain as president for another five years. Most press outlets described this referendum as bogus, and the six largest Islamic parties decided to boycott it,[25] especially since a month-long ban had been placed on political parties that had wanted to organise public rallies to protest the holding of the vote. More was to come. In August, the president enacted the Legal Framework Order (LFO), which contained constitutional amendments that further strengthened his power, and allowed him to dissolve the National Assembly under certain circumstances. It gave him authority to appoint the country's military chiefs and its Supreme Court justices, and led to the allotting of a certain number of seats for the military on the National Security Council, now designed to oversee not only strategic matters, but also those connected with 'democracy, governance, and inter-provincial harmony'.[26] Musharraf confirmed that the parliament would have no power to repeal the changes.

These constitutional amendments sparked a US rebuke of sorts, with a Department of State spokesperson describing the decisions as a barrier to the building of strong democratic institutions, and reminding Musharraf that 'free and fair national and provincial elections' due to be held in October were 'extremely important' to Pakistan.[27]

In a meeting between Bush and Musharraf in New York on 15 September, the US president apparently stressed to Musharraf the importance of Pakistanis following through on 'their commitments to return to full democracy'.[28] However, when he had been asked in August about the likely impact of Musharraf's constitutional amendments, Bush had stated that 'President Musharraf is still tight with us' in the struggle against terrorism and 'we want to keep it that way'.[29]

For the proclaimed US commitment to restoring democracy in Pakistan, therefore, much hinged on the elections that were due in October. As the Director of the Department of State's Policy Planning Staff, Richard Haass, put it after the poll, in a way that should have raised questions about the notion of Pakistan being 'tight with us', the more *complete* the democracy in Pakistan, the closer the working relationship was likely to be.[30] But, as Haass also acknowledged, the elections had not brought about completion. The ban on political rallies had been lifted six weeks before the polls, but there were allegations of harassment and vote rigging, and Musharraf's favoured party, the Pakistan Muslim League/Quaid-e-Azam, came out on top. Nevertheless, the actual outcome still retained elements that would shock leaders in both Washington and Islamabad. True, the Pakistan Muslim League/Quaid-e-Azam received the largest proportion of the votes and 25% of the seats. But the strong showing by a group of Islamic religious parties (the Muttahida Majlis-e-Amal (MMA) alliance) – which captured 20% of the seats – opposed to the US presence in the country and the leadership's support of the anti-terror operation, suggested the complexity of the political alignments in that country.[31]

US officials have subsequently tried to put a brave face on the election outcome. As Haass said: 'one of the things you have to understand is a democracy is when the people vote, the people vote. And what makes a democracy a democracy is that you can't control the results. Obviously, certain parties, including the MMA alliance did better than a lot of people predicted. So be it. That's how the people speak'. In testimony before Congress in March 2003, US

Assistant Secretary for South Asian Affairs Christina Rocca spoke more positively of the electoral process than was perhaps warranted, given that Musharraf retained the power to disband parliament and to remove the prime minister. While acknowledging that the elections were 'flawed', she averred that they did restore civilian government, 'including a Prime Minister and a National Assembly, after a three-year hiatus'. What she hoped for in future was the strengthening of democratic institutions and practices, especially a national assembly that could play a 'vigorous and positive role in governance and an independent judiciary that promotes the rule of law'.[32] This assessment was far more positive than the one in the Department of State's human-rights report published the same month. The latter stated that, although the elections had led to some limited powers being transferred to the parliament and prime minister, by the end of 2002, 'the assembly had met only twice and had not been permitted to debate any issues other than the Prime Minister's vote of confidence'.[33]

US policy designed to improve Pakistan's human rights record and its democratic practices has relied primarily on advocacy and economic aid. USAID has stressed the need for assistance to be directed especially to education, which it described as being 'in a critical state of disarray'. This is a reference to the need to reform the madrassas and other Islamic schools, which Bush approved in a statement following his June 2003 meeting with Musharraf. But USAID requested only $21.5m for this sector in FY03, whereas $200m has been allocated for emergency economic assistance,[34] and considerably more for security assistance. To date, the democracy promotion policy has yet to include a role for sanctions if the Pakistani government fails to meet any of its commitments in regard to democratic reform. Congress could hold up the $3bn pledged in June 2003, however, should it decide that Pakistan is failing to democratise, curb its support for North Korea, or to sustain its support for the struggle against terrorism.

US official statements on Islamabad rightly acknowledge that the restoration of democracy in Pakistan is at best a long-term project. Indeed, many US officials clearly understand that previous civilian governments in Pakistan had not necessarily served the country well and had presided over serious economic problems, ethnic and religious violence, and had tolerated high levels of corruption.

One result has been that, as USAID has put it, Pakistanis have 'often looked to the military during times of political crisis to serve as the government of last resort'.[35] When Musharraf first came to power he seemed to enjoy widespread popularity. Over time, though, his unwillingness to relinquish power and preference to consolidate it, combined with his decision to side with the US in the anti-terrorist campaign, have, in the former case, alienated those occupying the political middle ground, and, in the latter case, helped to forge consensus among the opposition religious parties that, unexpectedly, did so well in the October 2002 elections.

There is, therefore, a visible tension in US relations with Pakistan. The Bush administration describes its strategic interest as being to push Pakistan towards democratic, social and economic reform, while, at the same time, keeping it 'tight with us' and providing much-needed assistance in tracking down al-Qaeda. Those short-term goals appear to be triumphing over the trickier democracy objectives. The undercutting by Musharraf of the fragile institutions that could help Pakistan to become the kind of state that the US hopes eventually to nurture requires that Washington find a better balance between its twin lines of policy. As Teresita Schaffer has argued: a 'U.S. willingness to speak out against the army's manipulation of the political process in the months before the election might have strengthened the proponents of responsible and vigorous democracy and might have affected their attitude toward other U.S. policy goals'.[36] She advocates a greater percentage of US assistance being dedicated to bolstering Pakistan's institutions, such as the judiciary, the civil service and the parliament.[37] Above all, a policy focused almost exclusively on dialogue with Musharraf to the neglect of other political parties and leaders is not a recipe for promoting the preferred outcome of a moderate, democratic Islamic Pakistani state that is protective of human rights. As one US official is said to have told a *New York Times* reporter, the administration is aware that Musharraf's moves towards democracy are slow at best and that his political support is eroding.[38] Nonetheless, the Bush administration still went ahead and offered the general the accolade of a visit to Camp David.

Uzbekistan

Uzbekistan, with its 170-kilometre border with northern Afghanistan, and frontiers with four other Central Asian states, commands a vital geo-strategic location. With the US decision to overthrow the Taliban, its government quickly offered Washington access to its airspace and a base in the south of the country, at Karshi-Khanabad, which has reportedly accommodated about 1,000 members of the US Army's 10th Mountain Division. It also provided a channel for the delivery of humanitarian assistance to the Afghan population via the 'Friendship Bridge' at Termez – once used to transport Soviet soldiers, as well as military supplies to the Northern Alliance.[39]

Moreover, when they were a part of the former Soviet Union, all Central Asian states, including Uzbekistan, cemented their relations with Afghanistan, which intensified dramatically after the 1979 Soviet intervention. Apparently, almost all Central Asian military officers holding the rank of lieutenant colonel or higher served in Afghanistan during the Soviet occupation and thus presumably were in a position to share information useful to the US war effort in October 2001.[40] Additional intelligence may also have been made available from the substantial Uzbek minority in Afghanistan.

The immediate reasons for Uzbek President Islam Karimov's interest in joining the anti-terrorism coalition stemmed from domestic security needs. From the late 1990s, the Islamic Movement of Uzbekistan (IMU) had stepped up its military operations in the country with the goal of overthrowing the regime and creating a new Islamic state. In February 1999, for example, five bombs exploded in a coordinated attack in Tashkent, killing (according to different reports) between 16 and 28 people and wounding between 100 and 351 others. Government officials attributed these bombings to the IMU, which also collaborated with the Taliban and received funding from al-Qaeda.[41] These links led the US administration formally to designate the IMU a terrorist organisation, first in 2000 and again in 2002.[42] Beyond these immediate needs, Karimov is interested in finding a counterweight to Russian influence in the region.

The US first established diplomatic relations with Uzbekistan in 1992, shortly after the collapse of the Soviet Union. The goals of the Clinton administration were to foster regional security and economic cooperation through promotion of membership of NATO's Partnership for Peace programme and of the Central Asian Economic Community.[43] The US also supported Tashkent's membership of the Organisation for Security and Co-operation in Europe (OSCE). 1998 saw US joint training with Uzbek forces, organised by the US

Central Command, and, in 2000, US Secretary of State Madeleine Albright visited Uzbekistan and awarded the country $3m in assistance for counter-terrorism initiatives and border security. In October 2001, a *Washington Post* article reported that the two countries had been engaged in covert operations against Taliban leaders and Osama bin Laden at least a year before the 11 September attacks.[44]

Once Uzbekistan overtly joined the fight against the Taliban in October 2001, US aid that had been flowing at a rate of about $20–30m a year increased to more than $160m (in 2002). Over one-third of it was security related. The US modernised the Soviet-era military base at Karshi-Khanabad, delivered small arms, and paid for take-off and landing and for the use of air corridors. USAID programmes expanded, employing NGOs in activities that focus on primary healthcare, water resource management, the strengthening of what is described as democratic culture, and the promotion of small- and medium-sized enterprises.[45] In 1996, the IMF had suspended lending to Uzbekistan, and more or less withdrew in 2001. At the end of that year, though, it signed a 'Staff Monitoring Agreement' with the country, marking a new period of engagement.[46]

Other evidence of a warming of ties between the two countries came with Karimov's visit to Washington DC and New York City in March 2002, where he was received by Bush, Powell, some members of the US Congress, the President of the World Bank, James D. Wolfensohn, and certain US business leaders. During that visit, the two governments signed a 'Declaration on the Strategic Partnership and Cooperation Framework', which included cooperation in the areas of democratisation, the economy and security. With respect to the latter, the US pledged to 'regard with grave concern any external threat to the security and territorial integrity of the Republic of Uzbekistan'. In the event of a serious security threat, the US promised to consult urgently with the authorities in Tashkent, so as to 'develop and implement an appropriate response in accordance with US Constitutional procedures'.[47] The implications of this agreement are that the US administration has determined to engage in a long-term relationship with Uzbekistan. Because of its potential for a diversified economy, its natural resources, and its growing population, together with its geo-strategic location, the administration has viewed the country as central to regional security and regional economic development.

Meetings between Uzbek leaders and US officials, including the president, were occasions to 'express appreciation' for Uzbekistan's anti-terrorist support.[48] Indeed, during a visit to Tashkent in December 2001, Powell praised Karimov and the Uzbek people for their 'political courage' in assisting the US in its military campaign, promising to continue 'to remain engaged with them long after this crisis is over'.[49] US Secretary of the Treasury Paul O'Neill, in discussions with Karimov in Tashkent in July 2002, also thanked the Uzbek president and the Uzbek people for their support, and expressed his admiration for Karimov's leadership as his country embarked on economic transition, adding gratuitously: 'It's a great pleasure to have an opportunity to spend time with someone with both a very keen intellect and a deep passion about the improvement of the life of the people of this country'.[50]

Uzbekistan's human-rights record

O'Neill's comments were either made in irony, ill-informed or highly hypocritical, given what had long been known about the Karimov regime's human-rights record. Karimov has been in power since the Soviet era, became president following bogus elections in 1991, and since that time has concentrated on strengthening his position. He had his first term extended to 2000 in a 1995 plebiscite, and parliament voted to permit him to run again on the grounds that this extension did not represent a new term of office. In 2000, there were sham parliamentary and presidential polls, which the OSCE declined to observe on the grounds that, in the run-up to them, thousands of people had been imprisoned for their religious beliefs, no genuine opposition parties were allowed to campaign, and there was neither freedom of association, assembly nor opinion. In the presidential election of 2000, Karimov claimed to enjoy the support of 91.9% of the population. In late January 2002, he held a referendum to extend his period of rule to 2007. Some 92% of the population is supposed to have given its backing.[51]

Serious human-rights abuses in the country compound the absence of democratic rule. Torture is endemic, show trials commonplace, and there have been regular attacks on both religious and secular groups, as well as human-rights advocates. The levels of repression increased substantially after the February 1999 bombings in Tashkent, with practising Muslims being the main targets. Out of a total population of some 24m, there are estimated to be a minimum of 7,000 political and religious prisoners. According to a USAID report, Freedom House has regularly ranked Uzbekistan as having the lowest degree of political freedom that is possible according to its criteria.[52]

US human-rights policy

During the Clinton era, Human Rights Watch described his administration as being the major source of pressure on the Uzbek government – offering direct assistance to nascent human-rights NGOs, sending diplomats to monitor trials, registering official protests against the suspected use of torture, and Albright, among others, urging Karimov to make a distinction between those who wished to be left alone to practise their religion in peace and those who engaged in terrorism. Both the Department of State's *Country Reports on Human Rights Practices* and its annual *International Religious Freedom* reports were highly critical. Levels of assistance, however, had been rising steadily over these years.

Human-rights concerns have remained prominent in discourse on US–Uzbekistan relations, even in the period since 11 September. The *Country Reports* released in 2002 and 2003 employ some of the toughest language about any country, describing Uzbekistan as an 'authoritarian state with limited civil rights', elections that are 'neither free nor fair', and, despite constitutional guarantees, with no separation of powers. They record that the police and national security services engage in 'numerous serious human rights abuses', including the use of torture, harassment and beatings, leading to several deaths in custody. Prison conditions are bad, detention prolonged, arrests often arbitrary, and there is no due process. The government also 'severely restricts freedom of speech and the press'. Unsurprisingly, the overall judgement of the reports was that the Uzbek government's human-rights record 'remained very poor'.[53]

Other US agencies, such as USAID, concur with this description, and with few exceptions (see, for example, O'Neill's comment above), the US has frequently made reference to this appalling legacy of abuse. These criticisms come from various directions, including the US Commission on International Religious Freedom, the major human-rights NGOs, the US Congress, the US representative to the OSCE, as well as from the executive branch. During Karimov's meeting with Bush and Powell in March 2002, while the Uzbek leader was thanked for his support in the struggle against terrorism, he was not rewarded with a high-profile summit but kept largely behind closed doors. Both Bush and Powell stressed that improvements in relations with the US depended on improvements in Uzbekistan's human-rights record and made public pledges that the administration would not shrink from discussing these problems.[54] It was presumably deliberate, too, that the Declaration on the Strategic Partnership (signed on 12 March 2002) placed democratic and market reform at the top of its preamble. Its first article made reference to the requirement to strengthen rule of law, civil society, political institutions and democratic values in society, 'ensuring respect for human rights and freedoms based on the universally recognized principles and norms of international law'.[55] Only then did it go on to discuss the economic and security aspects of the relationship.

The message to the Karimov regime from Department of State officials has been particularly consistent and has clearly fitted within the human-security paradigm. Elizabeth (Beth) Jones, the Assistant Secretary of State for European and Eurasian Affairs, claimed on her return from the region in February 2002 that she had explained that genuine security and a long-term relationship with Washington involved more than military cooperation, it also included political and economic reform. As she put it to the Uzbeks and others: 'You can't expect to have stability in your country without job creation … without that, you are simply creating a generation of people who are so disaffected that they become easy targets for extremist organizations'. On the political front: 'If the people of this country feel they have no choices, feel they have no voice in determining their parliament, their president … those are the people, again, who are going to find a much more congenial time in extremist organizations. If you want to have the kind of security that we're talking about, we have to talk in terms of specific improvements in human rights activities, respect for human rights, and expanding democratic processes'.[56] Jones stated her belief that the increased frequency and intensity of the discussions with Uzbek leaders increased the opportunities for hammering home these arguments.

In July 2002, Lorne Craner, the Assistant Secretary of State for DRL, made his second visit of the year to Uzbekistan, where he repeated many of the same points in a policy line that he said had been set by Bush and Powell: if the United States was to have 'a deep and broad relationship with Uzbekistan, it [could] not just rest on a security foundation' but had to include reforms in 'both economic and political areas'.[57] Before a Senate subcommittee later that month, Craner reiterated the human-security argument: 'democratic states that respect the human rights of their citizens are anchors of stability and motors of prosperity'. In his view, it was not a question of balancing the competing interest of security and human rights, but a matter of 'mutually reinforcing goals'. In phrases that were to be reflected later in the NSS, he stated his government's conviction that societies that 'respect human dignity and the integrity of the person are societies that adhere to the rule of law and provide no opportunity for terrorism to take hold' or that can deal more 'effectively' with extremism. He also repeated the language of the Department of State's human-rights report – that Uzbekistan's record remained 'very poor', that the use of torture was widespread, the judiciary not independent, due process not respected, and that the road to improving these conditions was indeed long. He warned the leaders of Central Asian states that 'closer relations with the United States [brought] with it a heightened level of scrutiny'. This had already led in the case of Uzbekistan to enhanced levels of contact with institutions like the ministries of justice and interior, as well as the procurator general.[58]

Congressional activity with regard to Uzbekistan also helped to reinforce the consistency of this message, as well as serving to remind the executive branch that certain members of the legislature were going to put pressure on the administration if it failed to deal with Tashkent's human-rights problems. Senators Joseph Lieberman (Democrat, Connecticut) and John McCain (Republican, Arizona) led a bipartisan delegation to Tashkent in January 2002. While thanking the government and its people for their help in defeating the Taliban, Lieberman promised that the US was interested in a long-term relationship with the country, but that conditions would be attached. During the delegation's 'very frank' discussions with Karimov on democracy and human rights, he warned that there would be limits placed on US support to the country unless there was progress in these areas.[59] Testifying before the Congressional Commission on Security and Cooperation in Europe, on behalf of the Commission on International Religious Freedom, Nina Shea reminded congressional representatives of Uzbekistan's ghastly record of torturing, imprisoning and arresting thousands of peaceful Muslims who rejected the state's attempts to control the practice of their religion.[60] In response to her testimony, as well as to that of others, including four Uzbek human-rights activists, the Chairman of the Congressional Commission on Security and Cooperation in Europe, Chris Smith, confirmed that he had told Karimov during his visit to Washington in mid-March that he would fight to make future US aid to his country, and 'Permanent Normal Trading Relations' status, conditional on human-rights reforms.[61] Indeed, in July 2002, Congress passed an amendment to the Foreign Operations Appropriations Act (FOAA) that required that the administration report every six months on all security and military assistance to the Uzbek government. In addition, it made all supplementary aid conditional on 'substantial and continuing progress' in meeting the democracy and human-rights criteria outlined in the March joint declaration.[62]

This matter of conditioning aid has arisen in discussion of Uzbekistan far more than it has in the case of Pakistan. Shea, for example, demanded that the US government not be content with rhetoric about intended improvements, but instead look for 'concrete and discernible changes'.[63] Some journalists have been direct and persistent in their questioning on these issues.[64] When Jones gave a press briefing soon after her visit to the country in January 2002, she laid out the specific issues on which the US government expected progress, including access by the International Committee of the Red Cross (ICRC) to pre-detention centres, registration of human-rights NGOs, an invitation to the UN Special Rapporteur on Torture, Theo van Boven, to visit the country, and the need to establish proper mechanisms for free and fair elections.[65] Asked about the possible consequences if Uzbekistan were to fail to make progress towards these specific benchmarks, her response was particularly revealing. It showed the reluctance of governments to impose material sanctions when they are trying to promote human rights (as well as other policies) in both the short and long terms in their bilateral dealings with abusive governments: 'Here is the difficulty I have with consequences. It's a hard question. The consequence is … that we are in their office, in their face, all the time. It seems to me that it makes no sense at all that a consequence of Uzbekistan not cooperating on democracy and human rights is to cut our aid which goes to democracy and human rights groups'. There was little point either, she noted, in cutting the small-business investment programmes that were helping Uzbeks to sell their goods. Pressed again to explain what the Bush administration would do if the Uzbek leadership ignored its advice, Jones would not go beyond confirming that all agencies, 'especially our Pentagon and JCS [Joint Chiefs of Staff] colleagues', would make sure that democracy and human-rights matters stayed 'right in front of the agenda', because all in the administration had agreed that US programmes were interlinked.

Jones also pointed to the achievements in Uzbekistan to date – Tashkent had acquiesced to US demands to allow the ICRC access to pre-detention centres, offered an amnesty to about 800 political prisoners, punished a few law-enforcement officials found guilty of torturing to death a number of prisoners, and engaged in a 'civil conversation' about the importance of these and other US demands, such as the invitation to the UN Special Rapporteur for Torture and the registration of NGOs.[66] On the eve of Karimov's visit to Washington in March 2002 he did allow the registration of the Independent Human Rights Organisation of Uzbekistan (IHROU), and, by late June, his government had issued an invitation to van Boven. At the end of the year there were further releases of political prisoners and the government permitted van Boven's visit to go ahead. Powell used some of these small steps in August to press Congress to approve the award of $16m of supplemental aid, much to the disgust of Human Rights Watch, which noted that the certification of progress was premature, and that each of the positive moves was more than countered by acts of a wholly negative kind.[67] These steps, the NGO argued, hardly represented 'substantial and continuing progress'.

Neither did van Boven's remarks on leaving Uzbekistan make for comfortable reading. He told a news briefing that torture was 'systemic' in the country, and that the types of torture regularly employed by the police and security services 'included beatings, electric shocks, immersing the victim's head in water, and suffocation by plastic bags'.[68] His March 2003 report formally confirmed these remarks[69] and included a series of recommendations that administration officials were already on record as stating they would be pressing the Uzbek authorities to implement. During Jones' January 2003 visit to the country, she alluded indirectly to van Boven's comments. While thanking her 'Uzbek friends for their strong support and cooperation in the global war on terrorism', she first criticised Tashkent's backsliding on economic reform, noting its imposition of domestic and regional trade restrictions. She then pointed to her continuing concerns about human-rights abuses, including the 'gruesome deaths of prisoners in jail at the hand of their jailors', calling on Interior Minister Zokirjon Almatov to investigate how those deaths had occurred and to prosecute those found to be responsible.

Faced once again with a barrage of questions from sceptical journalists about the pace of economic and political reforms in the country, Jones reaffirmed her arguments made in February 2002: that the security of a country could not rest on military means alone, but had to include economic development and the treatment of citizens according to internationally accepted human-rights norms. She also repeated what she had said to the Uzbek cabinet and president: that the administration would keep on requesting that Tashkent take other steps on the democracy and human-rights fronts, even while she attempted to give the Uzbek leadership some credit for moves already made, such as registering one human-rights NGO, the December political amnesty, and the visitation rights extended to van Boven.[70]

US policy towards Uzbekistan since 11 September has been to reward – with economic and military assistance and a declaration on strategic cooperation – its help in the struggle against terrorism. However, there is also verbal criticism of Tashkent's repressive policies. The message from US governmental and non-governmental actors on the human-rights front has been consistently critical in tone. A number of factors explain the Bush administration's continuing attention – even enhanced attention – to the human-rights record of the Uzbek authorities. Past written and verbal statements detailing the horrific record of abuse are difficult to cast aside. The attacks on pious Muslims have been so widespread that uncritical support for the Karimov regime would lend credence to the critics who charge that Bush officials equate all Muslims with terrorism. Moreover, the US Congress, armed with material from human-rights organisations, the OSCE, and the US Department of State, has indicated relatively strong interest in monitoring Tashkent's record, as has the media, which has been forthright in its questioning of US officials on this topic.

The Bush administration, though, has not yet shown willingness to go much beyond verbal criticism of Tashkent and to use material leverage to ensure fuller compliance. A proportion of US aid is designed to contribute to human and not just state security, and it is understood that the goals set in the areas of political and economic reform are long term and uncertain. The IMU and al-Qaeda are still active in the region, and possibly preparing to attack US interests and citizens in Uzbekistan. Despite the requirements of security, however, a clear line can be drawn between the wide-scale abuse of human rights that is occurring inside Uzbekistan, and the means required to track down genuine terrorists. As yet, the US seems unwilling to draw that line, or only to draw it at the rhetorical level.

US failure to make this distinction and the absence of a policy that utilises political and economic levers to achieve specified improvements encourages Uzbek leaders to believe that they need move only slowly, or can get away with offering token gestures, while leaving the systemic structures of repression intact. After all, their domestic political agendas do not coincide very much with those of America. This serves to increase local and worldwide scepticism about US statements that a long-term relationship with the Uzbek regime depends on the country undertaking genuine reforms.

Conclusion

These two front-line states have clearly benefited in many different ways from their closer association with the US. A proportion of US political and economic support has been devoted to promoting human rights and democracy in these two states, but a large proportion of the aid has been security-related. However, it is plain to see that in neither case is Washington willing to use the leverage that its position gives it to push hard for improvements in human-rights protections inside these two countries. At present, the Bush administration relies primarily on discourse to try to promote democratic and human-rights reforms, with Uzbekistan clearly receiving a tougher message than Pakistan. Unlike Pakistan, which is at the centre of a number of extremely complex strategic and political issues, the basis for the relationship with Uzbekistan is somewhat less complicated, which helps to explain the difference in approach. In addition, there is a greater unity of view in the US about the poverty of the Uzbek government's human-rights record.

Chapter 4

Southeast Asia: the Second Front

Following the defeat of the Taliban regime in Afghanistan, the US quickly came to regard Southeast Asia as the second front in the struggle against terrorism. While the sub-region is undoubtedly home to a moderate form of Islam, there is also much political and religious violence, as well as the presence of Islamist groups with links to international terrorist networks. In October 2002, the US government – and shortly thereafter the UN Security Council Sanctions Committee – designated a radical Islamic group based in Indonesia, Jemaah Islamiah, a terrorist organisation. Together with other Southeast Asian Islamist groups, it seeks to establish a pan-Islamic realm that encompasses 'Indonesia, Malaysia, the Muslim areas of the Philippines and Thailand and, eventually, Singapore and Brunei'.[1] It has also planned and actually carried out attacks on US and other Western targets in the region, and has been associated with a major outrage in Bali, Indonesia, in October 2002, which claimed the lives of over 200 people and with a bomb explosion at the Marriott Hotel in Jakarta in August 2003. One plot foiled as a result of Singaporean action in December 2001 included the targeting of the US embassy and naval facilities in the country, along with a subway station used by US military personnel in Singapore.[2] Changi airport in Singapore was also the focus of a potential attack. Most of the 13 individuals arrested in connection with this plot allegedly were members of a local branch of Jemaah Islamiah; according to the Singaporean authorities, at least eight had received training in al-Qaeda camps in Afghanistan.[3]

These states, then, have become significant in new ways to the US since 11 September 2001 – providing intelligence, undertaking surveillance of suspicious groups, and, in some cases, watching over US freight craft and warships laden with military and other supplies for the war and post-war effort in Afghanistan.[4] They have become sources of concern, too, because they have been venues for contacts between al-Qaeda forces and other Islamist groupings. However, these countries are also incomplete democracies or semi-authoritarian, with governments that are sometimes prepared to use counter-terrorism strategies to suppress the political opposition. In the case of Indonesia, it has a military that might play an important role in counter-terrorism operations. But the armed forces have also been internationally condemned, and had US sanctions imposed on them in past years, particularly as a result of the brutal way in which they dealt with the independence movement in East Timor in the 1990s.

Indonesia

Indonesia has become crucial in the second wave of the struggle against terrorism for two key reasons. As the US Deputy Secretary of Defense, and former Ambassador to Jakarta in the 1980s, Paul Wolfowitz, has frequently remarked, Indonesia has the largest national Muslim population in the world – officially some 90% of a population in excess of 200m – but has been tolerant of other religions and has not had an established state religion.[5] It has also been undergoing a transition to democracy, propelled by the serious financial and economic crisis that it endured after 1997. While this transition is potentially a very positive development, more negatively, it has helped to leave it, in Wolfowitz's estimation, 'wide open' to terrorist activity. Its state institutions remain weak and levels of poverty and unemployment are high. Partly for these reasons, hardline Islamists have taken advantage and it has fallen prey to terrorist activity, at one stage allegedly having housed camps for the training of al-Qaeda groups.[6] The Indonesian Islamic teacher, Riduan Isamuddin ('Hambali'), arrested in August 2003 in Thailand, has been identified as a terrorist network leader. After the Bali bombings of October 2002, the Indonesian police arrested the Muslim cleric, Abu Bakar Bashir, accusing him of being the head of Jemaah Islamiah, and implicated this organisation in the Bali attacks. In September 2003 Bashir was finally acquitted of the central charge and jailed instead for sedition, receiving a four-year sentence.[7] The Bali bombings, in particular, forced Jakarta to crack down harder on terrorist groupings and to pass new anti-terrorism laws, bringing it closer into line with the policy priorities of the US.

What role the military should play in counter-terrorist operations and more broadly – at a time when Indonesia faces domestic and transnational terrorist threats – has been revived as a matter of major concern in Indonesia as well as in Washington. In the period after Indonesia's independence, the armed forces were closely associated with the country's identity and character.[8] The military played a hugely pervasive role in the life of the nation, well beyond that of most military institutions, especially after 1965 and the coup and counter-coup that eventually brought President Suharto to power under the New Order regime. Suharto, and those who propelled him into office, was 'profoundly anticommunist, obsessed with national unity, and preoccupied by perceived threats of subversion'. The regime came to power in a brutal manner and set in motion a 'culture of violence' that has strongly influenced the operation of the state itself, and the behaviour of the Indonesian military, including its much feared elite combat units, Kopassus and Kostrad.

The military's concept of *dwifungsi* ('dual function') reflected its belief that it had a legitimate political role to perform. Its strategy of 'total people's defence' implied close collaboration between the armed forces and the civilian population in order to defend the country against both internal and external threats. In addition, this provided it with a powerful intelligence network in all parts of the country. Not only did it play a key role right down to the village level, but its belief in *dwifungsi* also meant that it shaped the executive, legislative, bureaucratic, and judicial branches of the political system.

Its overweening power and customary modes of behaviour have been devastating for many within Indonesia. Wherever there were political movements demanding greater autonomy or independence – in Aceh, East Timor or West Papua, for example – the military employed unbridled tactics in its attempts to put these struggles down. Even beyond these areas, the armed forces acted with impunity, frequently resulting in systematic human-rights violations.

As an ardent anti-communist and the head of a country that is strategically located, Suharto enjoyed Western support for much of his first 25 years in power. US relations with Indonesia strengthened in the 1980s, including a tripling of US exports as the Indonesian economy expanded. As the Cold War began to draw to an end, though, international and US support started to decline, dovetailing productively with the growing confidence of domestic civil-society groupings dedicated to political reform and to achieving some accountability for past human-rights abuses. There were also divisions within the military along functional and generational lines that provided openings to civilians impatient to challenge the military dominance of society.

While the brutal governmental counterinsurgency campaign against the independence movement in Aceh from 1989 did not attract much international attention,[9] similar methods used against the East Timorese did. The massacre of an estimated 270 people in November 1991 at Santa Cruz, Dili, sparked a wave of domestic and international criticism that lasted throughout the 1990s, reaching a crescendo as a result of the military-directed violence that accompanied the East Timorese vote for independence in August 1999. The collapse of the Suharto dictatorship in May 1998 came as a consequence primarily of severe economic dislocation after the Asian financial crisis. With the advent of a democratic transition process, the new leadership in Indonesia embarked upon consolidating the movement towards civilian rule and retrenchment of the military: its representation in the legislature was cut by 50%, the police separated from the armed forces, and a civilian minister of defence was appointed. USAID programmes at this time were directed towards bolstering civilian oversight of the military, strengthening the capacity of civil-society organisations, and aiding the newly independent media. In 2000, USAID shifted its resources into 'conflict prevention, mitigation, and resolution activities in Indonesia's "Hot Spots"', including Aceh and West Papua. A precarious ceasefire was negotiated in Aceh in December 2002, but this broke down in April 2003, and, in May, President Megawati Sukarnoputri declared martial law and extensive military operations restarted. International observers were prevented from entering the province to observe the course of these operations.[10]

US human-rights policy before 11 September
The November 1991 killings in Dili moved the issue of human rights to a higher point on the US–Indonesia political agenda, with the

administration of US President George Bush calling for the punishment of those responsible for the outrage. Congress went further, however, legislating a termination of the International Military Education Training (IMET) programme for Indonesia in the FOAA for FY93. IMET had been in place since 1950 and more than 4,000 Indonesian military personnel had received training in the US. Jakarta had also received security assistance since 1950 (except during the coup period of 1965 and 1966) – grant aid for military equipment not being ended until 1978.

Under the Clinton administration, Indonesia continued to be criticised for its human-rights abuses in East Timor: the US representative to the United Nations Commission on Human Rights (UNCHR) introducing a resolution in 1993 condemning Jakarta's behaviour. However, sanctions in the 1990s mostly involved the IMET programme, with the US Congress often taking a harder stance than the executive branch. Congress reacted in 1995 to the Clinton administration's request to modify the ban on IMET for Indonesia, for example, by approving an Expanded IMET programme that would focus on human-rights training, and enhancing civilian control of the military. Participants in E-IMET would also include members of parliament and NGO representatives. Congress additionally imposed language in the FY95 FOAA that would prohibit the sale of 'small or light arms and crowd control items' until the secretary of state could determine that 'significant progress ha[d] been made on human rights in East Timor and elsewhere in Indonesia'.[11]

Further sanctions were to be imposed as a result of the large-scale military and militia violence that followed the East Timorese vote for independence in August 1999. Clinton announced the termination of most remaining contacts with the military, now called the Tentara Nasional Indonesia (TNI),[12] including commercial sales of military equipment. More significant and long-lasting, though, has been the amendment to the FOAA of 1999 introduced by Senator Patrick Leahy (Democrat, Vermont). That amendment restricted the resumption of IMET and US government-funded arms sales unless there was evidence that the Indonesian authorities were taking 'effective measures to bring to justice' military officers and militia members responsible for the major human-rights abuses that had occurred in East Timor.[13]

Despite this legislation, Indonesian officials were optimistic that the incoming Bush administration would lift the military sanctions. However, although members of the administration, as well as the US Pacific Command, supported lifting the ban, FY01 FOAA continued to forbid funding for IMET and Foreign Military Financing unless the Indonesian government met eight human-rights-related conditions.[14] It is this issue of accountability that has proven to be the main stumbling block to full restoration of ties between the US and the Indonesian militaries. The re-establishment of ties has been pressed especially strongly in the Pentagon since 11 September 2001.

US human-rights policy after 11 September

The International Crisis Group has rightly noted that any expansion of military-to-military relations between the US and Indonesia has taken on enormous symbolic rather than material importance. Such ties are largely viewed as a general 'barometer' of relations, and are representative of where human rights stand in US policymaking with respect to Jakarta. Shifts in US policy are capable of sending important signals about how seriously Washington takes the matter of military reform and how concerned it is about the TNI's current and past lamentable human-rights record.[15]

This debate about the full restoration of ties in broad terms has pitted an apparently united Pentagon against a somewhat less vociferous Department of State in alliance with some key members of the US Congress and international human-rights NGOs. Both sides have drawn support from different constituencies within Indonesia and in neighbouring countries, including the local NGO community and parts of the local and regional governmental elite. The argument for the restoration of ties has been made at two levels. The first rests on strategic questions of a short- and long-term nature. The Indonesian military is supposedly an important source of intelligence on regional and global terrorist networks. The country sits astride some of the world's major sea-lanes, and is a potential regional counter-balance to a rising China. The second line of argument is that it makes no sense to have had contact with the Indonesian military when it was operating under a dictatorship, but none while the country is democratising. This denies the Indonesian authorities, as Wolfowitz put it, the opportunity to 'bring their military to the U.S. where they can see officers engaged in a democratic government'.[16] In a November 2002 interview with Cable

News Network (CNN), Wolfowitz went further, hinting – although denying that it was straightforward 'cause and effect' – that problems with the Indonesian military had become worse over the ten years that the US had chosen to isolate it.[17]

Leahy, however, the prime mover in preventing the restoration of ties, continued in 2002 to argue passionately for the maintenance of restraints, noting that IMET had been provided for 47 years before the brutalities inflicted on the East Timorese and that US foreign aid had had to be used to rebuild East Timor 'after the army's destruction' of the country. He also noted that no military officer had been found guilty of the offences in 1999, and that the army was continuing to arm 'Muslim extremist militias' in other parts of the country, and was also involved in 'drug smuggling, prostitution, human trafficking, illegal logging, and many other illicit enterprises'. There was no evidence, he stated, of willingness to reform or to bring to justice those responsible for large-scale abuses.[18]

The 2002 and 2003 versions of the *Country Report on Human Rights Practices* supported Leahy's general argument, describing Indonesia's human-rights record as 'poor', and stating that the security forces were responsible for much 'indiscriminate shooting of civilians, torture, rape, beatings and other abuses, and arbitrary detention in Aceh, West Timor, Papua ... and elsewhere in the country'. The reports also note that the 'Government's critical failure to pursue accountability for human rights violations reinforces the impression that there would be continued impunity for security force abuses'.[19]

Despite these points, in July 2002, Senators Daniel Inouye (Democrat, Hawaii) and Ted Stevens (Republican, Alaska) introduced at a Senate Appropriations Committee Hearing an amendment seeking to lift restrictions on IMET for Indonesia in FY03. On 2 August 2002, Powell announced a $50m package to be expended on security and counter-terrorism between FY02 and FY04. The bulk of the money was destined to go to the police: $31m for training and assistance, and $16m to help establish a special police counter-terrorism unit. But $4m was set aside for regional counter-terrorism fellowships to provide training for the TNI,[20] and $400,000 for military training in FY03 under IMET.[21] In announcing this programme, the secretary of state tried to balance the importance of the proposal to resume IMET funding with a warning that the performance of the TNI would continue to be monitored to ensure that previous problems were 'dealt with and [that] there will be accountability'. He went on: 'We will measure this, and this will assist us in taking the case for further support to our Congress'. Powell also described this as 'just a beginning, and there are many stops along the way until we get to a full resumption of military-to-military activities and cooperation'.[22] Nevertheless, Powell's other statements showed how conclusively officials like Wolfowitz had shaped the argument on Indonesia: 'If you get young officers, expose them to a military organization that is within a democratic political institution, such as the United States, then that rubs off on them'.[23]

It was left to the US embassy to explain what accountability meant, describing the outcome of the ongoing human-rights trials of 18 high-ranking police, military and civilian officials indicted for their roles in the violence in East Timor as an 'important litmus test' of TNI accountability.[24] This did not convince many of Indonesia's NGOs, however. Demonstrating outside the US embassy in Jakarta, they reportedly argued that, for the army and the police, the aid 'provided political legitimacy [for the view] that they have been accepted back into the fold'. That acceptance also increased the possibility that intra-state conflicts would continue to be settled through means that trample on human rights.[25]

The outcome of the human-rights trials neither helped those concerned about accountability nor those wishing to restore full ties with the TNI. In August 2002, six military and police officers were acquitted. The last governor appointed by Jakarta to East Timor, Abilio Jose Osorio Soares, despite being convicted of crimes against humanity, received a sentence of only three years. One of the acquittals pertained to the former Regional Police Commander, Brigadier General Timbul Silaen, who had responsibility for security during the balloting for independence.[26] Three months later, four more were acquitted, including two former military commanders, although an ex-militia leader, Eurico Guterres, was jailed for ten years.[27] The Department of State described the outcome of the trials in August and November as disappointing, noting that the only convictions to date had been of East Timorese nationals, while the Indonesian security forces had not been called to account. Neither had the prosecutors made use of the extensive evidence of atrocities that the UN had compiled. It warned Jakarta that only 'effective and credible prosecutions' would lead to a 'closer relationship with Indonesia, including its military'.[28]

Only in late December 2002 was a military officer, Lieutenant Colonel Sujarwo, finally sentenced, but just to five years in jail for crimes against humanity.[29] That decision, subject anyway to appeal, could well have been connected to the fact that the US Congress that had been elected at mid-term in 2002 would consider the restoration of IMET funding on 24 January 2003. The congressional outcome was in fact mixed: the FY03 foreign-aid bill which finally passed through the Senate in February 2003 did confirm the $400,000 for IMET, but it also maintained human-rights conditions on the licensing and financing for export of military equipment to Indonesia. Bush would have to certify to the US Congress that military officers 'credibly alleged to have committed gross violations of human rights' had either been suspended or prosecuted for their crimes in order for that particular sanction to be lifted. (This broader wording covered not just actions in East Timor, but also incidents that were still occurring in provinces like Aceh and Papua.) However, the TNI's subsequent implication in the deaths in August 2002 of two Americans and one Indonesian teacher living and working in Papua led the Senate Foreign Relations Committee in May 2003 to reinstate the ban on IMET, until Bush certified that the Indonesian government was taking 'effective measures' to bring to justice those implicated in the killings.[30]

This delay in reinstating IMET funding is important, but it is now connected with the deaths of two Americans rather than the wider concerns about the TNI's role in committing human-rights abuses in East Timor and elsewhere. It is a symbolic but real test of a US willingness to stick to the path of promoting accountability for the past abuses of Indonesian security forces. In March 2003, the Deputy Assistant Secretary of State, Matthew P. Daley, had already admitted that the battle was all but over, affirming that the 'track record on accountability' was not good, but that, in order to influence the behaviour and attitude of the TNI and to protect American interests, the US had to 'interact with them'.[31]

A number of factors had been stalling military reform apart from the signs of support from the US Department of Defense – among them Megawati's belief that the TNI was the institution that could prevent any further break-up of the country; the lack of capacity of other civilian institutions; and the post-Bali sense that the army's intelligence networks could make an important contribution to the anti-terrorist struggle and had to be reactivated as part of a more general reassertion of its role.[32] Nevertheless, in the external realm, US policy as reflected in the determined statements by Wolfowitz,[33] which contributed to the steady erosion of the conditions that Washington had placed on resuming ties with the military, seriously undermined the idea that the security sector would be called to account for its past human-rights abuses.[34]

Malaysia

Malaysia, like Indonesia, is a majority Muslim state, but, unlike Indonesia, Islam is the official religion, and thus the political debate has not been about whether the country is secular or Islamic, 'but what kind of Islamic state it should be'. Dominated for more than 40 years by the ruling United Malays National Organisation (UMNO) coalition, in the late 1990s, there was a rise in political support for the Partai Islam SeMalaysia (PAS) connected to widespread domestic dismay following the arrest and conviction of former Deputy Prime Minister Anwar Ibrahim. The PAS now controls two of Malaysia's 13 states.[35]

Malaysia has become an important second-front state in the struggle against terrorism for both negative and positive reasons. Jemaah Islamiah established cells in Malaysia, one of which allegedly coordinated the plot to attack US and other Western installations in Singapore. Two of the hijackers involved in the 11 September attacks visited cell members in Malaysia in 2000; the Malaysian police videotaped their activities. The police turned the tape over to US intelligence officials who apparently placed their names on an immigration watch list, but failed to prevent them from entering the US.[36] Malaysian security officials have been relentless in arresting terrorist suspects. They also responded favourably to Powell's request that Kuala Lumpur host an Association of South East Asian Nations (ASEAN)-wide counter-terrorism centre – although there had been considerable sparring over the details. In May 2002, the two countries signed a 'Declaration on Cooperation to Combat International Terrorism', designed to enhance the exchange of intelligence information.

The US administration was grateful for the early political support of Malaysian Prime Minister Mahathir Mohamad, especially his statement that, whatever the cause, terrorism cannot be justified.[37] Immediately after 11 September, he gave concrete proof of his distaste for terrorism by visiting for the first time the US embassy in Kuala Lumpur where he signed the condolence book. During a visit to Kuala Lumpur in April 2002, Assistant Secretary of State James Kelly suggested further reasons why the US should deem cooperation with Malaysia important: 'as a moderate and predominantly Islamic country in Southeast Asia, Malaysia plays an important role in the global war on terrorism and is a beacon of stability in the region'.[38] Coincident with the anti-terrorist struggle, Malaysia has taken up leadership positions in major developing-world organisations, hosting the thirteenth Conference of Heads of State or Government of the Non-Aligned Movement (NAM) in February 2003, and acting as the head of the OIC in October 2003.

Mahathir, who finally retired at the end of October 2003, has been outspoken in his criticism of US foreign policy – towards the Palestinians, in Iraq, and even during the anti-Taliban campaign in autumn 2001. His statement at the NAM summit apparently almost resulted in the recall of the US ambassador to Malaysia. But at the working level, relations have long been steady: beyond cooperation in anti-terrorism operations, there have been important trading, military and educational linkages. The US is Malaysia's number-one source of foreign investment and its largest trading partner. It hosts 15–20 US ship visits a year and some 1,500 of its military officers have trained under the IMET programme.[39]

US human-rights policy before 11 September

US official statements on the human-rights situation in Malaysia have generally stressed its overall reasonable record, while noting significant problems in certain specific areas, such as with regard to freedom of assembly and expression, the police, the judicial system, and, especially, the inappropriate use of the Internal Security Act (ISA). US–Malaysian relations in this area of policy deteriorated markedly in autumn 1998 when Mahathir moved for political reasons against Anwar Ibrahim. After demonstrations in Kuala Lumpur in support of Anwar, he was arrested and charged with corruption and sodomy. Twenty-seven of his supporters were also detained under the ISA. While in custody, he was beaten up by former Inspector General of Police Rahim Noor.[40]

The trial procedure itself fell well short of international standards: the prosecutors amended charges during the trial; dates of the alleged offences were changed; the defence was not allowed to call certain witnesses; and prosecution witnesses allegedly were coerced into confessions damaging to Anwar's case. The court handed down a sentence of six years on four counts of corruption in 1999 and nine years on the charge of sodomy in 2000 – the sentences to be served consecutively.

In 2001, the government stepped up its use of the ISA, detaining six political activists in April associated with the opposition Partai Keadilan (National Justice Party) led by Anwar's wife, Wan Azizah Ismail. It was not until June 2003 that the six were all finally released. In August 2001, the police arrested ten members of an Islamic group, the Kumpulan Mujahidin Malaysia (KMM), under the ISA, some of whom were also members of the PAS.

Members of the US legislative and executive branches, together with various NGOs, reacted negatively to the developments in 1998 in part because of concerns about the abuse of Anwar's rights, but also because it proved to be a way of berating Mahathir for his anti-free-trade practices, use of capital controls, and insulting remarks about George Soros and others in the wake of the financial crisis that hit Asia in 1997. The Chairs of the House International Relations Committee and the House Asia and Pacific Subcommittee, Benjamin A. Gilman and Doug Bereuter respectively, wrote to Clinton, for example, on the eve of the APEC Summit due to be held in Kuala Lumpur in mid-November 1998. They argued that he should try to find an alterative venue, or if he did go, he should 'speak out forcefully about the economic policies and human rights practices of Prime Minister Mahathir'.[41]

For other reasons, Clinton did not attend, sending Vice-President Al Gore instead, where the latter duly spoke favourably of Anwar's supporters who were demonstrating in the streets.[42] Albright paid a call on Anwar's wife, despite a very tight schedule, where she voiced a 'lot of support' according to Azizah Ismail, and publicly stated her concerns about whether Anwar, 'a highly respected leader', would receive 'due process and a fair trial'.[43] These actions infuriated some members of the Malaysian political elite and led Mahathir to extend his open support for Bush's candidacy in the 2000 election.

When the Bush administration came to power in 2001, the Malaysian government clearly hoped that it would be able to mend relations at the highest level.[44] Mahathir made that clear to the US ambassador in Kuala Lumpur in early April. In all, prior to 11 September, at least three envoys were sent to Washington in an attempt to improve ties. The first ever meeting between a Malaysian foreign minister and a US secretary of state, while reported positively in the Malaysian press,[45] in fact resulted in Powell informing Syed Hamid Albar that improved relations and any possible meeting between Bush and Mahathir depended on how they treated Anwar and the opposition members detained under the ISA, and whether they stopped delaying the release of foreign news publications in Malaysia. Other branches of the US administration, such as the National Security Council (NSC), repeated the same message.[46] Indeed, according to the incoming US Ambassador to Malaysia, Marie T. Huhtala, the impact of Anwar's treatment internally and on US-Malaysian relations was 'a real watershed sort of event … a serious issue'. She affirmed that the Bush administration considered Anwar to be a political prisoner and that the US would continue to press its concerns about the opposition-party figures detained under the ISA.[47]

US human-rights policy after 11 September

Blocked by this tide of sympathy for Anwar and dislike of Mahathir in US official circles, the Malaysian government decided to try another less direct approach. This time it allegedly used – with considerable success – the connections between a Malaysian deputy minister and the Heritage Foundation, which was known to contain members close to Bush and his inner circle.[48] The Heritage Foundation helped to arrange to bring congressional staffers to Kuala Lumpur as the first stage in a move designed to establish a Malaysian caucus in Congress.[49] Heritage Foundation members and the Malaysian government recognised the strategic opportunity that 11 September offered, and moved quickly also to improve relations with the executive branch. Heritage apparently helped to establish contacts between Bush and Mahathir at the APEC meeting in Shanghai in October 2001, and to fix up a visit by Mahathir to Washington in mid-May. Some remaining concerns about the possible resurfacing of bilateral tensions during the May visit, however, led to a decision to send Malaysian Minister of Defence Najib bin Tun Abdul Razak to Washington ahead of Mahathir.

Najib's major speech in Washington, hosted jointly by the Heritage Foundation and the Center for Strategic and International Studies, reinforced the message that there had long been strong all-round cooperation between the two countries, particularly in the field of defence, and that there had been an 'elevated level of cooperation' after 11 September.[50] He also discussed the possible US sale to Malaysia of F-18E/F combat aircraft.

Mahathir's visit in May suggested that an adjustment had been made in the way that the Anwar issue would now be handled. Bush held a press conference with Mahathir after their meeting at which he stated that he wanted publicly to 'thank the Prime Minister for his strong support in the war against terror'. Apparently having failed to raise the matter of Anwar and the political detainees in his private meeting, Bush faced a journalist's query about whether his administration's position on these matters had changed. The president responded briefly that it had not.[51] Only in US media coverage did the Malaysian leader face somewhat tougher treatment, most notably in the *New York Times* which recorded the contrast between Bush's remarks on Cuba's human-rights record at the 14 May press briefing compared with the failure to make any reference to that of Malaysia. And during a CNN interview, Mahathir was forcefully quizzed on whether his government was using anti-terrorism and the ISA as a means of silencing his critics.[52]

Subsequently, remarks by, and the behaviour of, the Department of State suggested where the compromises would be made, even though the *Country Report* on Malaysia's human-rights record published in 2003 maintained the same tough language about Anwar and the political detainees. During Powell's visit to Kuala Lumpur in July 2002 he averred that he had raised human-rights issues in the three meetings that he had held with Malaysian officials (including with Mahathir) on 30 July, and had 'touched on' the Anwar issue. He also stated at a press conference that he believed Anwar's trial to have been 'flawed'. Rather than Powell meeting with Anwar's wife, as had been the case with Albright in 1998, Kelly met with her instead.[53] As Huhtala explained it, Bush administration officials would continue to speak openly and frankly about human rights and the Anwar case, but that case would no longer dominate a relationship that had over the previous year 'identified many areas of cooperation, where our interests overlap'. In her view, the relationship had 'moved on from the Anwar issue' and now both sides simply 'agreed to disagree'. US officials would still take the position that the 'trials were flawed', but they would not say that 'we support Anwar, or that reformasi is good for Malaysia'.[54] The US Deputy Assistant Secretary for East Asia and the Pacific, Matthew P. Daley, also recorded a further finely grained but significant shift in the US position on the ISA, stating that, while the ISA had been 'used to stifle domestic opposition', a distinction had to be made 'between that use and its current implementation in a counterterrorism context'.[55]

It is these kinds of statements that have prompted Malaysian officials to claim that the US government now recognises the value of the ISA, and that it shares many similarities with the USA Patriot Act.[56] The use of the ISA against PAS members has also come to matter less to US officials once alleged members of that party demonstrated outside the US embassy, expressing their sympathy with the Taliban and calling for a jihad against the US. The relative narrowness of US human-rights concerns regarding Malaysia, compared with so many other abusive governments, also has made it easier to put the Anwar and ISA issue to one side, especially since Malaysia has accomplished much in the Bush administration's view by tracking down terrorists and their networks in Southeast Asia.

Thus, it is only the lobbying of US and Malaysian human-rights organisations, backed sometimes by journalists willing to remind US officials of what they have written and said about these matters in the past, that will serve to keep the Anwar question and the inappropriate use of the ISA alive. The Department of State's *Country Report on Human Rights Practices* will also continue to provide ammunition for these and other groups and individuals. Perhaps Mahathir himself has also helped to maintain some attention to the issue as a result of his strident criticisms of aspects of US foreign policy, particularly its decision to go to war with Iraq.[57]

Conclusion

The human-rights-related issues that once shaped US relations with Indonesia and Malaysia have diminished in importance since 11 September. The bilateral relationships, as one US ambassador has put it, have moved on, in Indonesia's case largely as a consequence of a determined effort by the US Department of Defense to re-establish contacts with the Indonesian military, and in Malaysia's case because its help in tracking down terrorist groupings in Southeast Asia has taken precedence over inappropriate use of the ISA, or flaws in the trial of a former deputy prime minister. With the end of the long autocratic rule of Mahathir, the US Congress and administration is most likely going to be fixed on ensuring continuing cooperation in counter-terrorist activities, and on observation of the degree of steadiness in the political transition. Attention to the lamentable human-rights record of Indonesia, especially that of the TNI, rests on enough members of the US Congress, aided and informed by human-rights NGOs in the US and Indonesia itself, voting to retain legislative constraints. It also depends on how serious and how public are the abuses of the security forces, the main concern in this area now being the military's campaign in Aceh.

Chapter 5

China: A Third Front?

The Bush administration has not described China as a third front in the struggle against terrorism, but it is clearly an important participant in many different aspects of that struggle.[1] The Chinese leadership speedily offered its condolences to Bush following the events of 11 September and gave its support to UN Resolution 1368, recognising the attacks as a threat to international peace and security. As host of the APEC conference in Shanghai in October 2001 it helped to produce an official statement containing anti-terrorist sentiments; it encouraged Pakistan to work with the US and to support its fight against al-Qaeda and the Taliban regime; and it also agreed to a series of joint measures that, in other eras, would have been seen as far too intrusive. These measures have included regular meetings of the US–China counter-terrorism units dealing with financing and law enforcement; the establishment of a Federal Bureau of Investigation (FBI) legal attache's office in Beijing;[2] and the emplacement of US customs inspectors at Chinese ports to help with the inspection of US-bound cargoes.[3] China also has a small border with Afghanistan and longer ones with several Central Asian states, together with the Pakistani-controlled sector of Kashmir. Through the Shanghai Cooperation Organisation, China, Russia and the countries of Central Asia have been sharing information on entities perceived as threats to their regimes, and this has increased Beijing's capacity to offer intelligence to the US on regional Islamist groupings.

Beyond these matters directly related to 11 September, Bush administration officials did not find the Chinese government obstructive during the UN Security Council debates on Iraq, and helpful in dealing with the tensions that regularly arose between India and Pakistan in 2002. China has been playing a leading role in trying to broker the Six-Party Talks concerning North Korea's nuclear programme. With regard to weapons proliferation, while failures in implementation remain a serious problem from the US perspective, Beijing has promulgated new controls, modelled on Missile Technology Control Regime (MTCR) guidelines, on the export of technologies deemed useful to the production of weapons of mass destruction. Provided the trajectory remains positive, in the Bush administration's view, this warrants warmer US relations with China and permits Beijing to be considered as a potential member of a concert of powers that contributes to the maintenance of global and regional order at a time of great uncertainty. As Powell put it in a speech to the Asia Society in June 2002, the US wanted to work with China and encourage Beijing 'to make decisions and actions befitting a global leader. We ask China to collaborate with us and with our allies and friends to promote stability and well-being worldwide. To pressure governments that sponsor or harbor terrorists. To bring peace to regions in crisis. To become a global partner against poverty and disease, environmental degradation and proliferation'.[4]

US human-rights policy before 11 September

Human-rights issues, particularly in the period since the June 1989 bloodshed in Tiananmen Square, have been more prominent in America's relations with China than in all of the other examples chosen for this study. This was not the case, however, when Nixon first went to China in 1972. He stated that what had brought the US and China together at that time was 'recognition of a new situation in the world and a recognition on our part that what is important is not a nation's internal political philosophy. What is important is its policy toward the rest of the world and toward us'.[5]

During the 1970s, rather than paying attention to human-rights abuses in China, US administrations were primarily interested in China's economic-reform efforts and credit was given for its repudiation of past instances of large-scale abuse during the Maoist era. In addition, of course, China and the US were tacit allies in the struggle against the Soviet Union and this coincidence of strategic interest continued to be given priority in the relationship. When Vice-Premier Deng Xiaoping visited the US in 1979, Carter did raise concerns about religious freedom in China, constraints on those chosen to participate in educational exchange programmes, and travel restrictions that might be imposed on US journalists, but these concerns were not pushed firmly.[6]

Only as more Americans began to visit the People's Republic of China (PRC), including Tibet, and China became eligible for the US Foreign Military Sales Program, did this begin to change. A series of disturbances in Tibet from late September 1987 to early March 1989, culminating in the establishment of martial law, led Congressman Tom Lantos (Democrat, California), for example, to invite the Dalai Lama to Washington. Both houses of Congress pressed the Reagan administration to censure China for its behaviour in the province. These actions marked the start of broader public concern in the US about the Tibetan struggle for autonomy.

It took the bloody events of 4 June 1989, however, before large numbers of Americans would focus attention on China's human-rights record. The Chinese crackdown on the pro-democracy demonstrators attracted wide-ranging economic, military and political sanctions for a time, drawing together in cooperative action the US, its major allies and the IFIs. Nevertheless, the US government soon revealed, as did many others, that it was reluctant to sustain material sanctions (apart from on weapons sales) with a state as important as China. For one thing, it wanted China's support for, or acquiescence in, US-organised action in response to Iraq's invasion of Kuwait in 1990. For another, the administration understood that, only under the most exceptional circumstances, would the UN or any other grouping of countries intervene forcefully in such a state to protect the abused. And sustaining economic sanctions was seen as likely to impose sacrifices on the sanctioning country, especially when adopted against a nation as large and as potentially rich as China.[7]

During the Clinton era, following the breakdown in 1994 of the policy of trying to link human-rights improvements in China to 'Most Favoured Nation' trading privileges,[8] the main point of leverage was the US threat to frame a condemnatory resolution at the UNCHR. The US also held back from an agreement to organise official visits between heads of state in the absence of a Chinese commitment to sign the two major international human-rights covenants. US businesses were encouraged to agree to a voluntary code of conduct for their commercial operations in China. To some degree, this symbolic pressure on Beijing seemed to be effective, since China's signature of the ICESCR did come on the eve of President Jiang Zemin's visit to the US in October 1997.[9] In addition, China's promise that it would sign the ICCPR – which finally occurred in October 1998 – came on 12 March 1998, the day before Washington confirmed that it would not pursue a UNCHR resolution targeting Beijing. Clinton's return visit to China in June 1998 led to agreements to speed up a rule-of-law programme, and to revive the bilateral dialogue on human rights that had been suspended in 1995.

The US Congress mandated certain new requirements in the human-rights area during Clinton's last years in office. A US–China Relations Act of 2000 established a Congressional-Executive Commission to 'monitor China's compliance with international human rights standards, encourage the development of the rule of law, establish and maintain a list of victims of human rights abuses, and promote bilateral cooperation'.[10] The establishment of this body had helped to clear the way for the Clinton administration to win support for the terms of China's entry into the World Trade Organisation (WTO), and for China to receive 'Permanent Normal Trading Relations' status.

Matters of religious freedom also began to receive greater attention. In October 1998, Clinton signed into law the International Religious Freedom Act, which was passed unanimously in the House of Representatives and the Senate. That act mandated both the establishment of an Office of International Religious Freedom within the Department of State and an independent bipartisan US Commission on International Religious Freedom. It required the production of an annual report on the degree of religious persecution in various countries. Mirroring the style of the Department of State's *Country Reports on Human Rights Practices*, the parts of these reports that deal with China contain separate sections on Tibet, and address the oppression experienced by a number of religious groupings (including the spiritual-cum-meditative group known as Falun Gong).

Thus, apart from that immediate post-Tiananmen period, Washington's human-rights policy towards China came to be made up of the following two main strands: verbal shaming of China either at the UNCHR, in bilateral meetings between US and Chinese officials, or through Department of State and other reports by special US commissions set up for monitoring purposes; and some 'subcontracting' of the issue via the encouragement of US businesses operating in China to adopt codes of conduct in the workplace designed to advance health and labour rights, funding Radio Free Asia transmissions, and supporting NGOs that help to advance various 'rule-of-law' programmes inside China.[11]

When the Bush team entered office in January 2001, it held the view that the previous administration's stance towards China had generally been weak, and that Clinton had been less than candid when he had described the relationship as a 'strategic partnership'. As far as Bush was concerned, China was a competitor and should not be given 'friendly' attention at the expense of democratic and long-standing US allies like Japan and South Korea. In order to drive this latter point home, Bush made sure he received the South Korean and Japanese leaders before receiving China's Vice Premier Qian Qichen.[12] When Qian arrived, Bush apparently stressed that relations with China would be 'a lot easier' if only the authorities in Beijing would 'honor religious freedom within their borders'.[13]

The Bush administration, with strong congressional backing, soon made the decision (in 2001) to sponsor another draft condemnatory resolution at the UNCHR.[14] The resolution expressed concern about restrictions on 'the freedoms of assembly, association, expression, conscience and religion, and to due legal process and a fair trial'. It singled out constraints on Tibetans, arrests and sentencing of members of the China Democracy Party, the 'severe measures taken to restrict the activities of Buddhists, Muslims, Christians and others', as well as 'the increasingly severe measures taken against adherents of movements such as Falun Gong'.[15] Bush also took other steps to show his strong sympathy for the Tibetan cause: whereas Clinton had met with the Dalai Lama in June 2000 on an unscheduled, 'drop-by' basis, Bush met him in a scheduled and, therefore, better publicised meeting. Moreover, he chose to hold the meeting on 23 May 2001, a highly sensitive date marking the fiftieth anniversary of the signature by the Chinese government and the then local government of Tibet of the 17-point agreement of 1951, which formalised Chinese rule in the province. Beijing claims this agreement as the legal basis for its takeover of Tibet; the Dalai Lama's government-in-exile insists Beijing has grossly violated the accord. By meeting on that date, Bush helped to publicise the Dalai Lama's version of Tibet–China relations.[16]

Undoubtedly, these two developments reflected the personal and political predilections of a president whose religious faith is central to his identity. Another important factor has been the voting behaviour of the so-called Christian conservatives or 'religious right', 80% of whom voted for Bush in the 2000 election (as against 65% for Bob Dole in 1996), rallied to Bush's side over that of McCain in the primaries, and to some degree accounted for Gore's loss of his home state of Tennessee.[17] This grouping expects Bush to pay particular attention to religious persecution in China.

Despite this rocky start to the Sino-American relationship, including a new arms package for Taiwan, and then the crisis in April 2001 following the collision of a US surveillance plane and a Chinese jet, the administration started to develop a more nuanced policy towards China from mid-2001. As US administrations have come to realise, there are both coincidences as well as conflicts of interest in the relationship with Beijing, which give often turbulent relations a reason to rediscover some measure of equilibrium. Powell's visit to China in July – the first high-level member of the Bush administration to go to the country – symbolised this change in understanding. When Powell met with his Chinese counterpart Tang Jiaxuan, the two sides agreed – apparently at China's request – to resume the bilateral human-rights dialogue that had been suspended after the accidental US cruise-missile attack on the Chinese embassy in Belgrade during the Kosovo war in May 1999.

US human-rights policy after 11 September

As noted earlier, the US has been reasonably content with China's stance in the struggle against terrorism: the Chinese leadership was muted in its criticism of military action against the Taliban and Saddam Hussein, and continues to undertake 'careful monitoring of its borders with Afghanistan and Pakistan'. It regularly consults with US experts on the financial aspects of terrorism, and shares intelligence information on possible terrorist activities.[18] However, two factors have ensured continuing attention to China's human-rights record. First, China's determination to take advantage of the anti-terrorist struggle by equating all action in support of self-determination or greater autonomy within the Xinjiang Uighur Autonomous Region (XUAR) as terrorist, has tempered that American gratitude.[19] The Chinese government was extremely quick to produce a report linking acts of terrorist violence in the XUAR with Osama bin Laden and the IMU.[20] Yet, according to Dru Gladney, 'separatist and violent incidents in Xinjiang have dropped off dramatically since the late 1990s' and, despite the continuation of civil unrest, none of the strategic infrastructure targets in the province have been attacked.[21] The Chinese authorities have adopted an expansive definition of terrorism – for example, linking, in December 2002, a Tibetan religious leader, Tenzin Deleg Rinpoche, based in Sichuan to a series of bombings and sentencing him to death (suspended for two years) for having committed terrorist crimes. His co-defendant, Lobsang Dhondrup, was summarily executed.[22]

Second, the embedded nature of the human-rights issue in US–China relations – in the executive and legislative branches, among the US media, and in the vibrant non-governmental human-rights community – has also ensured continuing attention to China's human-rights record. The US administration has been especially concerned to press the message that it disapproved of Beijing's indiscriminate targeting of all Muslims in Xinjiang. It has also been important to Bush to signal to his domestic supporters that human rights, and especially matters of religious freedom, would influence the way he approached relations with Beijing.[23] In October 2001, at the APEC meeting in Shanghai, for instance, and in response to yet another wave of oppressive acts by Chinese security forces in the XUAR, Bush warned Jiang that the struggle against terrorism should not be used 'as an excuse to persecute minorities', adding later that 'ethnic minorities must know that their rights will be safe-guarded – that their churches, temples and mosques belong to them'.[24] During Bush's visit to China in February 2002, on the thirtieth anniversary of the path-breaking Nixon summit, his speech at Qinghua University gave considerable attention to matters of religious faith and freedom of opinion and assembly. Recalling the importance of faith in shaping his own life, Bush stated: 'Freedom of religions is not something to be feared but to be welcomed, because faith gives us a moral core and teaches us to hold ourselves to high standards'. Later he added (in language reminiscent of Clinton speeches): 'In a free society, diversity is not disorder. Debate is not strife. And dissent is not revolution. A free society trusts its citizens to seek greatness in themselves and their country'. He reminded his audience that 'China had an old tradition of tolerating all kinds of religions. My prayer is that all persecution will end, so that all Chinese people are free to gather and worship as they wish'.[25]

The US Ambassador in Beijing Clark Randt also promised greater and not less vigilance on human-rights matters. Just prior to the human-rights dialogue held between US and Chinese officials in December 2002, he claimed that he had demanded substantive results from the meeting, informed his audience, comprising members of the American Chambers of Commerce in Beijing, that he had 'continuously and persistently raised cases of prisoners of conscience as well as humanitarian cases involving victims of China's evolving legal system', and averred that 'no other single issue receives more of my personal attention'.[26] Neither is there much evidence from US Department of State *Country Reports* on China, together with those that deal with religious freedom, that the language has been toned down – in 2003, China, for example, was designated a country of particular concern in regard to religious persecution.

ETIM labelled a terrorist organisation

Nevertheless, the US decision in August 2002 to label the East Turkestan Islamic Movement (ETIM) operating in Xinjiang a terrorist organisation,[27] and subsequently to put it on a UN list that obliges all member states to freeze the group's assets and to deny its members entry to their respective territories, has been interpreted as a concrete quid pro quo for China's cooperation in the anti-terrorist struggle. So has the US decision of April 2003 not to sponsor a resolution critical of China at the annual session of the UNCHR.

With respect first of all to the ETIM, two related factors may well explain the designation of this group as terrorist in late August. First, the decision was announced during the August visit of Deputy Secretary of State Richard Armitage to Beijing, at the same time that China agreed to promulgate new missile-related export control regulations.[28] Second, the US was hoping that China would adopt a favourable attitude to any UN Security Council resolutions authorising the use of force to disarm Iraq.

Timing aside, however, the designation itself was already a near-certainty. From March 2002, US officials were stating that 'some Uighurs have been found fighting with al-Qaida in Afghanistan and we are aware of reports that some Uighurs who were trained by al-Qaida have returned [to] China'.[29] The 2001 report of the US Office of the Coordinator for Counterterrorism – produced in May 2002 – reiterated this statement.[30] Chinese Uighur separatists were picked up in Afghanistan during the campaign against the Taliban, and apparently a number are still being held in Guantanamo Bay. Reports in June confirmed that three Chinese Uighurs detained in Pakistan had been found with detailed maps of US embassies in Kyrgyzstan and Kazakhstan, and had been planning attacks on these sites. A US embassy spokesperson linked these three individuals with the ETIM.[31]

Moreover, prior to 11 September, the Chinese government allegedly had made contact with Taliban leaders on at least three occasions in an attempt to stop their support of certain groupings in Xinjiang. These contacts included a visit by Taliban officials to China, a trip to Kabul by members of a Chinese institute associated with China's Ministry of State Security, and another mission to Kabul by China's Ambassador to Pakistan in December 2000.[32]

If there are links between the ETIM and al-Qaeda, though, specialists on Xinjiang tend to agree that the ETIM is relatively small and weak, hardly constitutes an organisation and that China has seriously exaggerated its transnational significance and its level of influence on other Uighurs in Xinjiang.[33] Thus, having singled out and accepted the labelling by China of the ETIM as a terrorist organisation, the Bush administration has had to find a way to signal that it will continue to resist China's failure to distinguish between peaceful dissent and terrorist activity in the province. In the March 2002 statement, and on nearly all subsequent occasions, US officials make reference to the presence of peaceful Uighur dissidents and warn that Beijing should not seek to use the struggle against terrorism as an excuse to persecute particular religious and ethnic groups.[34] During Craner's visit to Xinjiang at the close of the December 2002 human-rights dialogue – a damage-limitation exercise because of the manner and timing of the ETIM designation and Beijing's subsequent attempts to condemn all Uighur separatists as terrorists – he again urged China not to use terrorism to go after a whole ethno-religious group.[35] In his speech at Xinjiang University on 19 December, Craner made a clear distinction between America's condemnation of the ETIM and US support for the 'peaceful people of Xinjiang', and recorded his dismay at China's disrespect for Uighur rights.[36]

The April 2003 UNCHR meeting

The US failure to sponsor an April 2003 UNCHR resolution targeting China also suggested that a Sino-American bargain had been struck, probably over Iraq, North Korea, and cooperation in the anti-terrorist struggle. However, the overt reasons for non-sponsorship were human-rights related: a few days before the US decision, Beijing invited a representative of the Dalai Lama to the capital to discuss the prospects for 'genuine autonomy' within China, and the day before the US decision four Tibetans detained in connection with the bombings in Sichuan were released from custody. In addition, US spokesperson Richard Boucher, while noting an array of human-rights problems in China, pointed to four improvements in 2002: Chinese commitments in December 2002 to invite UN special rapporteurs without conditions; the invitation to the US Commission on International Religious Freedom to visit China; reception of special representatives of the Dalai Lama in Beijing and Lhasa; and the release of a significant number of political prisoners.[37] China's subsequent failure to live up to a number of these commitments, however, has received considerable attention in the Bush administration. It raises the possibility of the US reinstating its policy of seeking a UN condemnatory resolution at the UNCHR meeting in 2004.

Conclusion

Since mid-2001, and especially since the terrorist attacks of 11 September, there has been closer strategic cooperation between the US and China, exemplified in the several meetings that have been held between top officials from both countries. Nevertheless, China's human-rights record has remained subject to critical scrutiny by the US and has absorbed much time and resources. Although the actual policy influence of human-rights ideas will remain limited (as it has in the past), human-rights groups in Congress and outside of it won, some time ago, 'the rhetorical war' with respect to China's record.[38] The US and transnational NGOs together with parts of the media remain as vigilant as ever, and those in the US Congress long committed to investigating China's record, not always for normative reasons, remain attentive. The human-rights policies of US administrations towards China have almost entirely relied on a mixture of exhortation and verbal shaming since the mid-1990s, the use of quid pro quos – such as high-level visits – in order to secure the release from prison of individuals of particular concern[39] (Tibetans, Christians, well-known political activists, and Chinese individuals with US citizenship), and subcontracting to NGOs involved in rule of law programmes. There does not seem to have been much of a retreat from this approach since 11 September 2001. Indeed, the current message to China is that Beijing and Washington have common interests that have lately served to bring them together. But only the sharing of values as well as interests will lead to a true and lasting partnership.[40]

Conclusion

The external human-rights policies of most of the world's governments are not particularly robust. It is rare for governments to impose tough material sanctions to enforce compliance with international norms, and rarer still for humanitarian motives to be uppermost in cases of external intervention in conflicts that result in gross human-rights violations. Nevertheless, the idea that states, especially democratic ones, should have a human-rights policy, and that international institutional mechanisms to monitor behaviour should be supported, has become an established part of international life. Several governments have also come to voice the sentiment that state, regional and even global security depends on a sense of being secure at the individual level. And in the period since the late 1980s, external intervention in another state on humanitarian grounds has been advanced as an argument more frequently than in the past.

Given that the international human-rights regime lacks tough enforcement mechanisms, and economic sanctions are not much used, more often than not governmental attempts at enforcement involve rhetorical exhortation in the hope of shaming a state into changing its behaviour. They might also involve the denial of certain symbolic political benefits, or the provision of positive inducements to bring about change. There are many examples where the threat of a condemnatory resolution at the UNCHR, or the refusal of a much-prized summit, or the offer of entry into a valued grouping (such as the European Union) can make a difference – sometimes a very modest difference, but at other times of a more significant kind.

At times, the US has been an actor of considerable consequence in the promotion of human rights. This is because of its power in the global system, strong belief in the superiority of its democratic way of life, and underlying confidence in its own self-image. It is striking and praiseworthy that it has long had bureaucratic and legislative measures in place that allow for human-rights matters to enter into the policymaking process, although not so praiseworthy that these have been treated so selectively. Many other countries have introduced similar legislation, or reinforced their own measures.

However, the attacks of 11 September 2001 have not left this area of policymaking unscathed. These attacks have had important effects on America's willingness and capacity to promote an external human-rights policy, and on its commitment to protect the rights of those who live within its boundaries, or have been taken into captivity as a result of the struggle against terrorism. This represents another seriously negative consequence of the adoption of counter-terrorist policies that are undoubtedly essential, but which need to be developed in such a way as to minimise their human-rights costs.

The cases chosen for this study nevertheless do illustrate the complexity that is behind the measurement of the impact of counter-terrorism on America's external human-rights policy. There are five main instruments that the US has used over the years to promote human rights abroad:

- its own example;
- positive inducement;
- rhetorical shaming;
- material and symbolic sanctions; and
- military intervention (not relevant to the cases examined in this paper).

In none of the five Asian countries examined here have material or symbolic sanctions of much significance been sustained on human-rights grounds and the US capacity to promote rights by example has been significantly damaged as a result of actions taken in Guantanamo Bay and at home. Indeed, in three of the cases (Indonesia, Pakistan and Uzbekistan), while sales of some armaments have been prohibited, and some funding has been made loosely conditional on improvements in the areas of democracy and human rights, most sanctions have been removed since 11 September. Each country has received significantly increased levels of assistance. True, some part of that aid is directed at building state institutions to improve the protection of human rights, but the levels of security assistance often overshadow it. Political and military contacts have been increased, too, which can be taken as important sources of legitimation for these regimes. Where aid is not much a part of the US relationship – as with China and Malaysia – enhanced levels of contact have been of political benefit to particular leaders and their governments. And in all five cases, governments have taken the lead from the US in more frequently using, passing or strengthening their own internal anti-terrorism legislation, using this to crackdown on opponents, some of whom may be terrorists, but others who are clearly not. In these respects, therefore, the conclusion is that the struggle against terrorism has had, overall, negative consequences on the credibility of America's human-rights policy towards these states.

However, when it comes to rhetoric – an important component of human-rights promotion – the US has differentiated among the five governments. The harshest messages have been delivered to Uzbekistan and China, even though the former has been regarded as a front-line state in the counter-terrorist struggle, whereas the latter is less central. More nuanced arguments have been advanced in respect of Pakistan, Indonesia and Malaysia. Indeed, at the level of discourse (written and verbal), the evidence suggests that greater attention is paid to the Uzbek human-rights record post-11 September than before. There is also a consistency in the US view about the seriousness of the problems with the Uzbek government's human-rights record – in the US executive and legislative branches, among the media, and in the NGO community. Tashkent's behaviour is described as very poor and it has been informed, in written agreements and verbally on several occasions, that a longer-term relationship with the US depends on it undertaking fundamental political and economic reforms. In this case, US policy goes somewhat beyond rhetoric because Congress has imposed human-rights conditions on the release of supplemental funding, although it has not proven at all difficult so far for the executive branch to breach that legislative barrier.

Where China is concerned, the US has long described its human-rights record as poor, and latterly as improving in certain circumscribed areas. Much as in the past, though, the administration states that it will continue to deny Beijing a close and more equal relationship until it stops persecuting various of its peoples, especially those wishing to practise their religion in peace. In fact, in most respects, there is rather little difference between the Clinton and Bush administrations' policies towards China in the human-rights field – except for the greater emphasis now on religious matters – or between Bush administration policies pre- and post-11 September. Human-rights questions have impinged on Sino-American relations since the late 1980s and have become a concern to many official and non-official actors in the US. There is unlikely to be much in the way of significant change in this area of US policy unless China itself undergoes significant change.

Pakistan and Indonesia are described as embarking on democratic transitions that are capable of improving human-rights protections in the two countries. However, US policymakers understand that this transition process is fragile, lengthy and fraught with potentially negative as well as more positive consequences. In the case of Pakistan, some members of the US Congress are disturbed about the closeness of ties with a military-led government, as are members of the media; but it is recognised, too, that previous civilian administrations seriously failed the country. Elections do not always bring the desired results either. The stakes are extremely high with Pakistan: not only is Islamabad crucial to ongoing action against al-Qaeda, but its nuclear weapons are presently in the hands of a weak government, and it has a record of having assisted another country's nuclear-weapons programme. Furthermore, anti-Americanism in the country remains prevalent and Islamist sentiment strong. Pakistan also has an intractable dispute with India that could lead to catastrophic war. Thus, US exhortations that Pakistan move to civilian rule and improve human rights and democratic practices have been couched in language that is relatively muted and may not be deemed to be serious. Its penchant for singling out Musharraf for special support, rather than reaching out to a wider political community, is counterproductive to its goals of strengthening civil and political institutions.

What happens to the Indonesian military is central to the success of the democratic transition in that country, and is also seen in the US as crucial to the anti-terrorist struggle. Key figures in the Pentagon, especially Wolfowitz who is projected as something of an expert on the country, have forcefully shaped the discourse on what

US policy towards Jakarta and the TNI should be. The US Congress still acts as a partial bar on closer US relations with the Indonesian military; but Wolfowitz's capacity to influence policy has been enhanced because Congress has become more divided since 11 September on whether the security sector should be held to account for past human-rights abuses, or whether a fresh start should be made with the TNI. The idea of a 'fresh start' has more or less won out, pending the outcome of the FBI investigation into the deaths of two Americans in August 2002. Human-rights conditions have otherwise remained in place only in relation to some military sales, although it seems unlikely that these will stay intact for long.

The stakes, undoubtedly, are less high in the case of Malaysia, which generally has a better record on human-rights and democracy than the other nations analysed here. Kuala Lumpur's use of the ISA to round up suspected terrorists, as well as some political opponents, has become for Washington more a matter of congratulation than dismay. Its apparent efficiency in arresting alleged terrorists contrasts favourably with what has been happening inside Indonesia, although Jakarta, too, has become more active after the Bali bombings. The Anwar issue has distressed some US officials and a few members of Congress, and the failure of his appeal against sentence in April 2003 has been described as a 'deep disappointment'.[1] Mahathir's statements have often grated, but the country is not a major congressional or NGO concern. These understandings have made it relatively easy for the Bush administration to 'move on' from the main human-rights-related issues that interfered with the bilateral political relationship before 11 September, while maintaining some of the stock phrases to describe the problems associated with the Anwar case.

As noted earlier, human-rights dialogue is not unimportant in bringing about some improvements in the behaviour of abusive governments. Uzbek leaders agreed to a series of small steps in an attempt to demonstrate that they were committed to reform – releasing some political and religious prisoners, registering a human-rights NGO, and allowing van Boven to visit. Around the time of the Sino-American human-rights discussions of December 2002, China issued a blanket invitation for several UN special rapporteurs to visit, showed more interest in negotiating with the Dalai Lama's envoys, released a number of political prisoners (especially Tibetans), and accepted congressional funding for some 'rule-of-law' projects. Pakistan went ahead with elections for a national assembly and appointed a prime minister, even if Musharraf tried to massage the results beforehand. The Indonesian tribunal finally sentenced two military officers for crimes in East Timor, although these prosecutions still might not stick on appeal. These are, however, relatively minor adjustments at this point, and where the apparatus of repression remains in place, they are palliatives rather than indications of a fundamental change in thinking and behaviour. If the US were to combine dialogue with conditioned larger negative or positive material and symbolic incentives these steps would be more significant.

Analysis of these cases confirms that it is too straightforward to assume that, when a state is central to the anti-terrorist struggle, US attention to its human-rights record diminishes accordingly. Certainly, that factor is important, as the material on Indonesia, Malaysia and Pakistan indicates. However, where the US executive and legislature are not united – either singly or in combination – in their disapproval of a state's record, or in their understanding about how best to satisfy a range of policy goals, as with these same three states, this too can lead to a diminution in concern about human-rights abuses. Where there is a relatively unified view about the problematic nature of a state's human-rights record, as is true of China and Uzbekistan, then human-rights matters, at least at the discursive level, retain a prominent place in that state's relationship with the US.

These findings argue for a deeper debate in the US about how and where to strike the balance between the needs of security and the protection of human rights and civil liberties at home and abroad. The domestic and external realms are in fact inter-related, the credibility of the externally directed human-rights message being influenced by what is happening inside the US. If US officials are serious when they assert that human rights and security are 'mutually reinforcing goals', they need to be sure that the human-rights trade-offs are not made in areas recognised as non-derogative – the use of torture being a case in point. The trade-offs have to be limited to what is essential, and scrutinised to diminish opportunistic behaviour. They have to be projected as exceptional and, in some areas, as temporary measures. Otherwise, it is inevitable that the costs associated with the violence perpetrated by terrorist groupings will continue to be made larger still.

Notes

Introduction

[1] Quoted in Lorne W. Craner, Assistant Secretary of State for Democracy, Human Rights and Labor, 'Balancing Military Assistance and Support for Human Rights in Asia', Testimony before the Subcommittee on Central Asia and the Southern Caucasus, Senate Foreign Relations Committee, Washington DC, 27 June 2002, US Department of State Press Release.

[2] See, for example, D. Priest, and B. Gellman, 'US decries abuse but defends interrogations', *The Washington Post*, 26 December 2002, p. A1, and the letter to Deputy Secretary of Defense Paul Wolfowitz sent by the US Lawyers Committee for Human Rights and signed by nine heads of human-rights organisations (dated 14 January 2003).

[3] Such developments are discussed in T. Carothers, 'Promoting Democracy and Fighting Terror', Foreign Affairs, January–February 2003, pp. 84–91.

[4] B. Chellaney, 'Fighting Terrorism in Southern Asia: The Lessons of History', *International Security*, winter 2001/02, vol. 26, no. 3, pp. 94–116, especially p. 97. Chellaney refers to the US Department of State report, *Patterns of Global Terrorism – 2000*, (Washington DC: Office of the Coordinator for Counterterrorism, Department of State, April 2001).

Chapter 1

[1] *The Military Balance 2001•02* and *2002•03* (Oxford: Oxford University Press for the International Institute for Strategic Studies (IISS), 2002 and 2003), p. 15 and p. 241 respectively.

[2] J. Fallows, 'The Military Industrial Complex', *Foreign Policy*, November/December 2002, p. 47.

[3] The new department is described in *The Economist*, 23 November 2002, pp. 25–29.

[4] For further details about Abu Sayyaf and other local rebel groups, some of which have transnational terrorist links, see C.A. McNally, and C.E. Morrison, (eds), *Asia Pacific Security Outlook 2002*, (Tokyo: Japan Center for International Exchange, 2002), pp. 138–139, and 'Insurgency and Terror in the Philippines', IISS *Strategic Comments*, vol. 9, issue 4, June 2003.

[5] For the implications of this act, see 'A Year of Loss: Reexamining Civil Liberties since September 11', (New York: Lawyers

Committee for Human Rights, 5 September 2002), www.lchr.org/us_law/loss. The American Civil Liberties Union has also drawn attention to a draft legislative proposal known as PATRIOT II. See 'Right–Left Comes Together over Privacy, Civil Liberties Post-9/11', 10 April 2003, www.aclu.org/news/.

6 D. Cole, *Enemy Aliens: Double Standards and Constitutional Freedoms in the War on Terrorism* (New York: the New Press, 2003), p. 25.

7 E. Lichtblau, 'US Inspector General Report Criticises Significant Problems of Round of Immigrants after 9/11', *The New York Times*, 3 June 2003, p. A1.

8 *Human Rights Watch World Report 2002* and *Human Rights Watch World Report 2003* (New York: Human Rights Watch, 2002 and 2003), pp. 487–489 and pp. 499–504 respectively.

9 D. Cole, 'Fight Terrorism Fairly', *The New York Times*, 19 October 2002, p. A31. Federal District judges that have challenged these various denials of rights have either been defied by the Department of Justice or their judgements have been overridden on appeal. See editorial in *The New York Times*, 10 September 2002, p. A30. E. Alden, 'Pentagon will let detainee see lawyer for the first time', *Financial Times*, 4 December 2003, p. 11.

10 H.H. Koh, *The Nation*, accessed via www.time.com on 10 October 2002.

11 N. A. Lewis, 'More Prisoners to be Released from Guantanamo, Officials Say', *The New York Times*, 6 May 2003, p. A21.

12 John Mackinlay writes that these 'damning prisoner photographs were not taken by a paparazzo camera commando, but by US Marine photographers for a Republican home audience that wants to see the boot of retribution being applied'. He also argues that there are serious repercussions for troops everywhere that are open to capture: 'While these perceptions of US conduct might erode the moral confidence of [UK] servicemen and women in far-flung posts, they strengthen their adversaries and potential captors. The truth is no longer important; the goggles, gloves and blindfolds become an accusation which licenses captors to behave badly'. See J. Mackinlay,'Vulnerable', *The World Today*, March 2002, p. 16.

13 *Washington Post, op. cit.*, 26 December 2002, p. A1.

14 'U.S. Sidesteps Charges of Mistreating Detainees', Human Rights Watch news, 17 April 2003.

Chapter 2

1 M. Ignatieff, 'Is the Human Rights Era Ending?' *The New York Times*, 5 February 2002, p. A25.

2 'Farewell Speech in Geneva by Mary Robinson, United Nations High Commissioner for Human Rights', supplied by the Office of the High Commissioner, 12 September 2002.

3 J. Donnelly, *International Human Rights*, (Boulder: Westview Press, 1998), p. 15.

4 David P. Forsythe writes that human rights have 'a permanent but ambivalent status in US foreign policy'. See D.P. Forsythe, 'US foreign policy and human rights', *Journal of Human Rights*, vol. 1, no. 4, December 2002, p. 518.

5 This section relies on my *Rights Beyond Borders: the Global Community and the Struggle over Human Rights in China*, (Oxford: Oxford University Press, 2000), especially pp. 42–48.

6 J.I. De Neufville, 'Human Rights Reporting as a Policy Tool: An Examination of the State Department Country Reports', *Human Rights Quarterly*, 8/4,

1986, p. 682.

7   M. Keck, and K. Sikkink, *Activists Beyond Borders: Advocacy Networks in International Politics*, (Ithaca: Cornell University Press, 1998), pp. 10–11.

8   'Promoting Democracy in the Aftermath of September 11', statement by Carl Gershman, President, National Endowment for Democracy, to the Senate Subcommittee on Foreign Operations, 6 March 2002. The same argument can be made in the area of human-rights promotion. However, many governments outside the US do not necessarily see such bodies as truly non-governmental.

9   US reluctance to tie itself to various parts of the international human-rights regime is explained in R. Foot, 'Credibility at Stake: Domestic Supremacy in U.S. Human Rights Policy', in Y.F. Khong, and D.M. Malone, (eds), *Unilateralism and U.S. Foreign Policy: International Perspectives*, (Boulder: Lynne Rienner, 2003), pp. 95–115.

10 A. Roberts, 'The So-Called "Right" of Humanitarian Intervention', *Yearbook of International Humanitarian Law*, vol. 3, spring 2002, especially p. 12. The nine cases, in date order, are Northern Iraq, Bosnia and Herzegovina, Somalia, Rwanda, Haiti, Albania, Sierra Leone, Kosovo, and East Timor.

11 Of course, there is a much longer historical association between the US and the promotion of such ideas, as well as a great deal of controversy about the application and reasoning behind them. For a valuable text on democracy promotion, see M. Cox, G.J. Ikenberry, and T. Inoguchi, (eds), *American Democracy Promotion: Impulses, Strategies and Impacts*, (Oxford: Oxford University Press, 2000).

12 'Memorandum of Understanding between the Department of Defense and the Agency for International Development on the Conduct of Overseas Civil-Military Relations Programs', made available to the author by the OTI in November 2002.

13 The literature on this concept of human security is extensive. For a useful overview, see F. Osler, Hampson and J.B. Hay, 'Human Security: A Review of the Scholarly Literature', report produced for the Human Security Centre, University of British Columbia, Vancouver, http://www.liucentre.ubc.ca/hsq, accessed in October 2002.) For a sceptical view of the concept see, Y.F. Khong, 'Human Security: A Shotgun Approach to Alleviating Human Misery?' in *Global Governance*, vol. 7, 2001, pp. 231–236.

14 A valuable discussion of UN-authorised treatment of humanitarian operations under Chapter VII provisions is contained in J.M. Welsh, 'From Right to Responsibility: Humanitarian Intervention and International Society', *Global Governance*, vol. 8, 2002, pp. 503–521.

15 President George W. Bush, State of the Union Address, 29 January 2002, www.whitehouse.gov/news/releases/2002/01.

16 A useful catalogue of such statements is contained in H. Kim, '"Substantive Disagreements" on North Korea between Presidents Kim and Bush: Its Background, Contents and Meanings on South-Korea-U.S. Relations', prepared for the Korea–UK Forum, Clare College, University of Cambridge, 6 April 2002, especially pp. 21–27. During his February 2002 summit in Seoul with President Kim Dae Jung, Bush explained in a press conference that he had used the

phrase 'axis of evil' because 'I love freedom. I am troubled by a regime that starves its people, that is closed and untransparent; and I am deeply concerned about the people of North Korea'. H. Kim, '"Substantive Disagreements" on North Korea between Presidents Kim and Bush: Its Background, Contents and Meanings on South-Korea-U.S. Relations', *op. cit.*, p. 26. See also the translation of Bush's interview with three Asian countries on 16 February, in which he emphasises the lack of basic freedoms in North Korea. *Foreign Broadcast Information Service (FBIS)*–East Asia, 'Daily Report', 17 February 2002.

[17] See S. Chesterman, 'Humanitarian Intervention and Afghanistan', in J. Welsh, (ed), *Humanitarian Intervention and International Relations: Theory and Practice*, (Oxford: Oxford University Press, 2003) chapter 9. Bush remarked one year after the military campaign against the Taliban regime had begun: 'It's very important for our citizens to remember that as we upheld that doctrine that said, if you harbor a terrorist, you're just as guilty as the terrorists, that we went into Afghanistan to free people … and so we are helping the people to now recover from years of tyranny and oppression … to claim its democratic future, and … to establish public order and safety'. The president added: 'We will stay the course to help that country develop'. See 'US Humanitarian Aid to Afghanistan', The White House, Office of the Press Secretary, 11 October 2002.

[18] Foreign assistance is supposed to be raised by $5bn by 2006, which represents a 50% increase compared to the $10bn in the foreign aid budget in 2002. For a list of some of the countries that might benefit under this scheme, and how they might score across the range of criteria, see M. Hiebert, 'More Aid, But New Strings', *Far Eastern Economic Review (FEER)*, 20 February 2003, pp. 12–14.

[19] What Edward Rhodes has described as 'Wilsonianism with a vengeance'. See his article entitled 'The Imperial Logic of Bush's Liberal Agenda' in *Survival*, vol. 45, no.1, 2003, p. 133.

[20] M. Ignatieff, 'The Courage of Strangers', published in *Australian Financial Review*, 5 July 2002, p.1.

Chapter 3

[1] B.L. LePoer, 'Pakistan–US Relations', Congressional Research Service (CRS) Issue Brief for Congress, 31 December 2001. See also T.C. Schaffer, 'U.S. Influence on Pakistan: Can Partners have Divergent Priorities?' in *The Washington Quarterly*, vol. 26, no. 1, pp. 170–171.

[2] *Human Rights Watch World Report 2001*, (New York: Human Rights Watch 2000), p. 216.

[3] Mohan, C.R., 'A Paradigm Shift Toward South Asia?' *The Washington Quarterly*, vol. 26, no. 1, winter 2002/03, p. 144.

[4] S. Ganguly, 'India and Pakistan in the Shadow of Afghanistan', *Current History*, April 2002, p. 147.

[5] D. Sanger, 'Bush Offers Pakistan Aid, but no F-16s', www.nytimes.com/2003/06/25/international/asia/.

[6] S. Ahmed, 'The United States and Terrorism in Southwest Asia: September 11 and Beyond', *International Security*, vol. 26, no. 3, winter 2001/02, p. 84.

[7] A. Koch, and U. Farooq, 'Washington, Islamabad Strengthen Ties', *Jane's Defence Weekly*, 20 February 2002.

[8] F. Bokhari, 'Arrest signals determination by Pakistan', *Financial Times*, 3 March 2003,

p. 7, and A. Rashid, 'The Net Tightens on Al Qaeda Cells', *FEER*, 13 March 2003, pp. 12–14, which reports that Mohammed was found in a Rawalpindi suburb – the home to many within the Pakistani military – in a house owned by the brother of an army officer.

9   'Rocca Outlines U.S. Assistance to South Asia', US Senate Foreign Relations Committee, 26 March 2003, www.uspolicy.be/Issues/foreignpolicy/rocca.

10 Pakistan Horizon, 'Chronology', vol. 55, nos. 1 and 2, January–April 2002, 14 February 2002, p. 197; S.P. Cohen, 'The Nation and the State of Pakistan', *The Washington Quarterly*, vol. 25, no. 3, summer 2002, p. 116; 'President Bush Welcomes Pakistan's Commitment to Fighting Terrorism', 12 January 2002, www.whitehouse.gov/news/releases. The US viewed Musharraf's television address as highly significant in light of Pakistani support for militants operating in the part of Kashmir controlled by India and Islamabad's decision to ban four extremist organisations, including two that were accused of the attack on India's parliament on 13 December 2001 that killed 14 people. However, the speech came after the attempted bombing of the Indian parliament and mainly in response to a build-up of troops on the Indo-Pakistani border. Moreover, this 'permanent' stop to infiltration has since proved to be illusory.

11 'Remarks with President Pervez Musharraf of Pakistan', Secretary of State Colin L. Powell, Islamabad, 16 October 2001, www.state.gov/secretary/rm/2001/.

12 S. Ahmed, 'The United States and Terrorism in Southwest Asia: September 11 and Beyond', *op. cit.*, p. 85.

13 *Ibid.*

14 'Pakistan', United States Agency for International Development (USAID), www.usaid.gov/regions.

15 *Human Rights Watch World Report 2003, op. cit.*, p. 267. As of September 2001, Pakistan's total foreign debt stood at $37bn. S. Ahmed, 'The United States and Terrorism in Southwest Asia: September 11 and Beyond', *op. cit.*, p. 85.

16 *Human Rights Watch World Report 2003, op. cit.*, p. 267.

17 J. Harding, 'Musharraf wins $3bn aid pledge from Bush' *Financial Times*, 25 June 2003, p. 7.

18 See, for example, the reports of various human-rights organisations, especially the *Human Rights Watch World Reports, op. cit.*

19 *Country Reports on Human Rights Practices – 2001*, 'Pakistan', US Department of State, 4 March 2002, www.state.gov/g/drl/rls/hrrpt/2001.

20 *Human Rights Watch World Report 2003, op. cit.*, p. 267; *Country Reports on Human Rights Practices – 2002*, 'Pakistan', US Department of State, 31 March 2003, www.state.gov/g/drl/rls/hrrpt/2002.

21 'Letter to Secretary Powell regarding the U.S. State Department's Trafficking Report', Human Rights Watch, 18 June 2002, www.hrw.org./press/2002/06/powell-ltr. Also see *Country Reports on Human Rights Practices – 2002, op. cit.*

22 See, for example, Representative Eni Faleomavaega's remarks at a Hearing of the Subcommittee on Asia and the Pacific of the House International Relations Committee, 'The United States and South Asia: Challenges and Opportunities for American Interests', 20 March 2003.

23 'Remarks with President Pervez Musharraf of Pakistan', Secretary

of State Colin L. Powell, *op. cit.*

24 'U.S.–Pakistan Affirm Commitment Against Terrorism', 13 February 2002, www.whitehouse.gov/news/releases/2002.

25 See A. Rashid, 'Give Me More', *FEER*, 18 April 2002, p. 19 ; 'Musharraf's Risky Gambit' *Newsweek*, 13 May 2002, p. 2.

26 *Human Rights Watch World Report 2003, op. cit.*, pp. 260–261.

27 'U.S. sees Pakistani changes as new barrier to democracy', www.CNN.worldnews, 22 August 2002.

28 Agence France Presse, via LexisNexis, 15 September 2002.

29 *Human Rights Watch World Report 2003, op. cit.*, p. 267.

30 'Interview by Syed Talat Hussain of Pakistan Television', Islamabad, 31 October 2002, www.state.gov

31 T.C. Schaffer, 'U.S. Influence on Pakistan: Can Partners have Divergent Priorities?' *op. cit.*, p. 178.

32 'Interview by Syed Talat Hussain of Pakistan Television', *op. cit.*; 'United States Relations with South Asia', Christina Rocca, Testimony before the House International Relations Subcommittee on Asia and the Pacific, Washington DC, 20 March 2003, www.state.gov/.

33 *Country Reports on Human Rights Practices – 2002*, 'Pakistan', *op. cit.*

34 'Pakistan', USAID, *op. cit.* Moreover, in August 2003 more liberal access for Pakistan's textiles to the US market was refused. F. Bokhari, 'US rejects Pakistan plea on textile quotas', *Financial Times*, 13 August 2003, p. 8.

35 'Pakistan', USAID, *op. cit.*

36 T.C. Schaffer, 'U.S. Influence on Pakistan: Can Partners have Divergent Priorities?' *op. cit.*, p. 178.

37 *Ibid.*, p. 180.

38 See www.nytimes.com/2003/06/25/international/asia/.

39 'Uzbekistan emerges as key to allied effort', *Jane's Defence Weekly*, 10 October 2001; 'Central Asia and the war on terrorism', IISS *Strategic Comments*, vol. 7, issue 10, December 2001.

40 'U.S. Relations with Central Asia', Beth Jones, Assistant Secretary for European and Eurasian Affairs, Washington DC, 11 February 2002, www.state.gov/p/eur/rls.

41 'Central Asia's New States: Political Developments and Implications for U.S. Interests', Issue Brief for Congress by the CRS, Library of Congress, Washington DC, 6 January 2003.

42 See Richard Boucher's press statement, US Department of State, 25 September 2002, www.state.gov/r/pa/prs.

43 P. Jones Luong, and E. Weinthal, 'New Friends, New Fears in Central Asia', *Foreign Affairs*, vol. 81, no. 2, March/April 2002, pp. 61-70. See also C.W. Maynes, 'America Discovers Central Asia', *Foreign Affairs*, vol. 82, no. 2, March/April 2003, pp. 120–132.

44 G. Feifer, 'Uzbekistan's Eternal Realities: A Report from Tashkent', *World Policy Journal*, vol. 19, no. 1, spring 2002, p. 85.

45 'Uzbekistan', USAID, www.usaid.gov/country/ee/uz/ (updated 29 May 2002).

46 *Ibid.*; *Human Rights Watch World Report 2003, op. cit.*, p. 390.

47 'Declaration on the Strategic Partnership and Cooperation Framework between the United States of America and the Republic of Uzbekistan', signed 12 March 2002 (released 8 July 2002), US Department of State, www.state.gov/p/eur/rls/or/.

48 D. Milbank, 'Uzbekistan thanked for role in war', *Washington Post*, 13 March 2002, p. A23.

49 'Powell, Karimov Joint Press Conference in Uzbekistan', 8 December 2001, US Department of State, http://usinfo.state.gov/topical/pol/terror/.

50 Paul H. O'Neill, Secretary of the

Treasury, 'Joint Press Conference with President Islam Karimov of Uzbekistan', 17 July 2002, www.state.gov/e/eb/rls/.

51 *Human Rights Watch World Report 2001, op. cit.*, p. 337; A. Tabyshalieva, 'Human Rights and Democratization in Central Asia after September 11', Nordic Institute of Asian Studies, Copenhagen, *Nordic Newsletter*, no. 3, September 2002, p. 16; G. Feifer, 'Uzbekistan's Eternal Realities: A Report from Tashkent', *op. cit.*, pp. 82–83.

52 'Uzbekistan', USAID, *op. cit.* See also various *Human Rights Watch World Reports* and US Department of State *Country Reports on Human Rights Practices.*

53 *Country Reports on Human Rights Practices – 2001, 'Uzbekistan'*, 4 March 2002, and *Country Reports on Human Rights Practices – 2002*, 'Uzbekistan', 31 March 2003. The 2002 report adds: 'although there were some notable improvements, it continued to commit numerous serious abuses.'

54 *Washington Post, op. cit.* 13 March 2002, p. A23.

55 'Declaration on the Strategic Partnership and Cooperation Framework between the United States of America and the Republic of Uzbekistan', especially Article 1.2, *op. cit.*

56 'U.S. Relations with Central Asia', press briefing by Beth Jones, *op. cit.*

57 'Democracy and Human Rights in Uzbekistan', Lorne W. Craner, Assistant Secretary for the Bureau of Democracy, Human Rights and Labor, Media Roundtable, Tashkent, 7 June 2002, www.state.gov/g/drl/rls.

58 'Balancing Military Assistance and Support for Human Rights in Asia'", Lorne W. Craner, *op. cit.* Assistance Secretary of Defense J. D. Crouch also stated while testifying before the Subcommittee on Central Asia and the Southern Caucuses that Uzbekistan's levels of security and prosperity would only be enhanced as levels of democracy increased. See 'Central Asia: Washington Seeks to Balance Security, Human Rights', *Radio Free Europe/Radio Liberty*, 1 July 2002, www.rferl.org/nca/features/.

59 'U.S. Senatorial Delegation Press Conference in Uzbekistan', 6 January 2002, http://usembassy.state.gov/posts /pk1/.

60 'U.S. Policy in Central Asia and Human Rights Concerns', Briefing of the Commission on Security and Cooperation in Europe, 107th Congress, 2nd Session, 7 March 2002.

61 J. Donovan, 'Central Asia: Human Rights Activists Urge Tougher U.S. Stance', *Radio Free Europe/Radio Liberty*, 29 March 2002, www.rferl.org/nca/ features.

62 *Human Rights Watch World Report 2003, op. cit.*, pp. 389–390.

63 The steps that she had in mind included: releasing and stopping the arrest of 'persons imprisoned solely because of their religious beliefs, practices, or choice of religious association; ending torture; ... and refraining from using registration requirements to prevent religious groups from practicing their faith'. Briefing of the Commission on Security and Cooperation in Europe, *op. cit.*

64 They have also been direct with Karimov himself. During Powell's visit to Tashkent in December 2001, a CNN journalist asked the Uzbek president: 'what do you say to your critics who say that you are nothing more than a brutal, repressive, authoritarian dictator?' See 'Powell, Karimov Joint Press Conference in Uzbekistan', *op. cit.*

65 'U.S. Relations with Central Asia', press briefing by Beth Jones, *op.*

cit. These areas of improvement had been suggested by such human-rights organisations as Human Rights Watch.

66 *Ibid.*

67 *Human Rights Watch World Report 2003, op. cit.*, pp. 382–390, especially p. 389.

68 'Uzbekistan: UN Rapporteur says Torture "Systemic"', *Radio Free Europe/Radio Liberty*, 6 December 2002, www.rferl.org/nca/features/.

69 The UN Special Rapporteur presented his report at a special NGO briefing at the UNCHR on 4 April 2003. 'Uzbek Government Should Stop Torture', Human Rights Watch news, 4 April 2003.

70 'Assistant Secretary of State for European and Eurasian Affairs Visited Tashkent', press conference, 24 January 2003, www.usembassy.uz/2003/.

Chapter 4

1 A.M. Rabasa, 'Political Islam in Southeast Asia: Moderates, Radicals and Terrorists', *Adelphi Paper*, no. 358, IISS, May 2003, p. 9.

2 'East Asia Overview', *Patterns of Global Terrorism – 2001*, (Washington DC: Office of the Coordinator for Counterterrorism, Department of State May 2002), www.state.gov/s/ct/rlspgtrpt/2001/.

3 A.M. Rabasa, 'Political Islam in Southeast Asia: Moderates, Radicals and Terrorists', *op. cit.*, p. 60.

4 M.J. Hassan, 'Terrorism: Southeast Asia's Response', 3 January 2002, *Pacific Forum CSIS*, PacNet 1, via e-mail from pacforum@hawaii.rr.com.

5 'Deputy Secretary Wolfowitz Interview with Brown Journal of World Affairs', News Transcript, 8 April 2002, www.defenselink.mil/news/. The US *International Religious Freedom Report 2002* on Indonesia records that the Ministry of Religious Affairs has officially recognised five major faiths: Buddhism; Catholicism; Hinduism; Islam; and Protestantism. Legal provisions also state that other religions are not forbidden. See www.state.gov/g/drl/rls/irf. When Bush met with President Megawati Soekarnoputri in Jakarta in October 2003 the two agreed that Indonesia showed that 'democracy and Islam can go hand in hand.' 'Bush, Indonesia's Megawati Denounce Linking Terrorism and Religion', 22 October 2003, http://usinfo.state.gov/xarchives/

6 'Southeast Asia's Fragile States', IISS *Strategic Comments*, vol. 9, issue 2, 2003. See also T. Huxley, 'Disintegrating Indonesia? Implications for Regional Security', *Adelphi Paper*, no. 349, IISS, July 2002, pp. 77–78 for a fuller discussion of Indonesia's place at the heart of Southeast Asian terrorism.

7 D. Djalal, 'Landing the Big Fish', *FEER*, 27 February 2003, p. 19. In this article, Indonesian specialist Sidney Jones of the International Crisis Group describes Bashir as 'the social linchpin of the network, the person who connects everybody else'. See also J. Wagstaff, 'Cold Comfort', *FEER*, 11 September 2003, p. 18.

8 This next section draws extensively on G. Robinson, 'Indonesia: On a New Course?' in M. Alagappa, (ed), *Coercion and Governance: The Declining Political Role of the Military in Asia*, (Stanford: Stanford University Press, 2001), pp.226-256.

9 Robinson records that, between 1989 and 1998, about 2,000 civilians died in the Aceh campaign and 'countless others … [were] arbitrarily detained, tortured, and raped'. *Ibid.*, p. 240.

[10] See www.usaid.gov/country/ane/id/. I am also grateful to Chris O'Donnell, the Asia Team Leader in the OTI, Bureau for Democracy, Conflict and Humanitarian Assistance, USAID, for his willingness to share information on the Indonesian programme. (The interview took place in Washington DC in November 2002.) For details on the ceasefire and its subsequent breakdown, see: 'Moves to ease Aceh Violence', 16 April 2003, http://news.bbc.co.uk/1/hi/world/asia-pacific; and 'Indonesia: Conditions Decline in Aceh', Human Rights Watch news, 5 June 2003.

[11] L. Niksch, 'U.S.–Indonesian Relations', CRS Report, Library of Congress, number 94-233F, 13 June 1996, obtained via Center for Defense Information, www.cdi.org/issues. Indonesia was also pressured to improve labour rights or to suffer the removal of lower duties on US imports of Indonesian products via the US General System of Preferences.

[12] Before April 1999, the armed forces (then combined with the police) were known as Angkatan Bersenjata Republik Indonesia (ABRI).

[13] This bill is discussed in 'Congress Affirms Restrictions in U.S. Military Assistance to Indonesia', East Timor Action Network media release, 19 November 1999, www.etan.org/legislation.

[14] The International Crisis Group has produced a very helpful report, including an evaluation of the eight conditions. See 'Indonesian-U.S. Military Ties', ICG *Indonesia Briefing Paper*, 17 July 2001, www.crisisweb.org.

[15] *Ibid*, p. 1.

[16] P. Wolfowitz, 'Making Friends, Taking Aim', *FEER*, 20 June 2002, p. 24.

[17] 'Deputy Secretary Wolfowitz Interview with CNN International', 5 November 2002, www.defenselink.mil/news/Nov 2002.

[18] Senator Patrick Leahy, 'Remarks on Amendment on Indonesia Foreign Operations Bill Markup, Senate Appropriations Committee', 18 July 2002, http://leahy.senate.gov/press/. Representative Chris Smith has also been vocal in his criticism of attempts to restore funding, querying Admiral Dennis Blair in February 2002 whether his advocacy of this position circumvented 'Congress' clear intent that the US withhold training and assistance for the Indonesian military until its human rights record improves'. See 'U.S. Security Policy in Asia and the Pacific: The View from Pacific Command', Joint Hearing, 107th Congress, 2nd session, 27 February 2002, p. 54.

[19] *Country Reports on Human Rights Practices – 2001*, 'Indonesia', US Department of State, 4 March 2002, www.state.gov/g/drl/rls/hrrpt/2001/, and *Country Reports on Human Rights Practices – 2002*, 'Indonesia', US Department of State, 31 March 2003, www.state.gov/g/drl/rls/hrrpt/2002/. The quotes are taken from the 2001 report. Similar language is used in the 2002 report, although there is a slight softening of tone. Indonesia was also placed in the third tier (the worst possible ranking) in the Department of State's *Trafficking in Persons* report, and the 2002 human-rights report refers to trafficking as still a significant problem.

[20] Three Indonesian officers arrived at the Naval Postgraduate Training School in Monterrey, California, in late September 2002 to participate in this training programme. The three were apparently vetted by the US

embassy in case there was evidence of involvement in human-rights abuses. Interview with US official in the Department of State, Washington DC, November 2002.

21 'Summary of Counterterrorism Proposals for Jakarta', Fact Sheet, Office of the Spokesman, Jakarta, 2 August 2002, US Department of State, www.state.gov/r/pa/prs/ps/.

22 'Remarks with Indonesian Coordinating Minister for Political and Security Affairs Susilo Bambang Yudhoyono', Secretary of State Colin L. Powell, Jakarta, 2 August 2002, US Department of State, www.state.gov/secretary/rm.

23 'Powell treading a thin line in rallying antiterror support', *New York Times*, 31 July 2002, p. A7.

24 'US-Indonesian military ties far from normalized, says ambassador', *Deutsche Presse-Agentur*, 7 August 2002, via LexisNexis.

25 *FBIS–East Asia*, 'Daily Report', 15 August 2002.

26 'Indonesia: East Timor trials deliver neither truth nor justice', Amnesty International, 15 August 2002, http://web.amnesty.org/ai/nsf/. J. Perlez, 'Indonesia Finds Ex-Governor Guilty in East Timor Killings', *The New York Times*, 15 August 2002, p. A7.

27 *FBIS–East Asia*, 'Daily Report', 29 November 2002; J. Perlez, 'Indonesian Human Rights Court Acquits 4 in East Timor Killings' *The New York Times*, 1 December 2002, p. A10.

28 'Indonesia – Human Rights Tribunal for East Timor', US Department of State, 19 August 2002, http://usinfo.state.gov/cgi-bin/.

29 S. Donnan, and T. Hidayat, 'Indonesian officer convicted for East Timor abuses' *Financial Times*, 28 December 2002, p. 8. In August 2003, Major-General Adam Damiri was sentenced to three years in prison for 'crimes against humanity' but is also free pending appeal. 'A Rare Conviction for East Timor Crimes', *FEER*, 14 August 2003, p.10.

30 The US Federal Bureau of Investigation (FBI) has been brought in to investigate; the TNI carried out two inconclusive investigations of its own. J. McBeth, 'Enter the FBI', *FEER*, 13 March 2003, p. 22; 'A Message to Jakarta and Bush', *FEER*, 5 June 2003, p. 8.

31 'US Interests and Policy Priorities in Southeast Asia', testimony of Matthew P. Daley, Deputy Assistant Secretary, Bureau of East Asia and Pacific Affairs, to House International Relations Committee, 26 March 2003, www.uspolicy.be/Issues/foreign policy/daley.

32 On these latter points, see 'Impact of the Bali Bombings', *ICG Indonesia Briefing Paper*, International Crisis Group, 24 October 2002, www.crisisweb.org.

33 Interviewees in Washington DC in November 2002 stated that the various public statements made by the Deputy Secretary of Defense in the US and in Indonesia, especially around autumn 2001, had reinforced the sense within the TNI that it need go no further in reforming itself.

34 As one of the USAID documents has put it: 'In May 2002, the domestic and international macro-context is less supportive of wide-ranging military reform than at any other point of the post-New Order period'. This has led to an inevitable hindering of its own programmes in this domain. See 'Civil-Military Programs: Indonesia', 19 June 2002, www.usaid.gov/democracy/cmr/indonesia.

35 A.M. Rabasa, 'Political Islam in Southeast Asia: Moderates,

Radicals and Terrorists', *op. cit.*, pp. 39–40.

[36] Remarks by Ambassador Ghazzali to the Pacific Basin Economic Council (PBEC)'s US Annual Policy Conference 2002, p. 3, www.pbec.org/us/2002/.

[37] See, for example, Mahathir's speech to the member states of the Organisation of the Islamic Conference (OIC) in Kuala Lumpur, April 2002.

[38] 'Mahathir welcome in United States as Washington shifts focus', *Associated Press*, 15 April 2002.

[39] 'US Interests and Policy Priorities in Southeast Asia', statement by Matthew P. Daley, Deputy Assistant Secretary, Bureau of East Asia and Pacific Affairs, to the House International Relations Committee, *op. cit.* 'Rumsfeld praises Malaysia's efforts in war on terror', *Malay Mail*, 3 May 2002.

[40] The police chief pleaded guilty to beating Anwar, received a sentence of two months, but was released after 40 days for good behaviour. See *Country Reports on Human Rights Practices – 2001*, 'Malaysia', 4 March 2002.

[41] 'Reps. Gilman, Bereuter Letter on APEC Leaders' Meeting', 16 October 1998, US Department of State, http://usinfo.state.gov/regional/ea/apec/gilmanlt. The Heritage Foundation also turned out to be a supporter of Anwar – at least in 1998 – on similar grounds. 'The President and his administration should send a strong message to Mahathir regarding both his political treatment of Anwar and his economic policies that violate free-market ideals. They should seek a change in venue for the summit and publicly speak out on Anwar's situation.' See R.D. Fisher, Jr., 'Malaysia after the Crackdown: A Poor Venue for Asian Summit', *Executive Memorandum*, no. 557, 16 October 1998, www.heritage.org.

[42] As Gore put it to business leaders: 'Democracy confers a stamp of legitimacy that reforms must have in order to be effective. And so, among nations suffering economic crises, we continue to hear calls for democracy and reform in many languages, people's power, doi moi, reformatsi. We hear them today, right here, right now, among the brave people of Malaysia'. Mahathir accused him of inciting lawlessness. See 'The Malaysian Question', *Online NewsHour*, 17 November 1998, www.pbs.org/newshour/bb/asia/july-dec98/malaysia.

[43] 'Albright snubs Malaysia', *BBC News-World*, Asia-Pacific, 15 November 1998, http://news.bbc.co.uk/1/hi/world/asia-pacific.

[44] See, for example, 'Mutual respect essential for good relations', *New Straits Times*, 12 January 2001, p. 11.

[45] 'US welcomes Malaysia's intention to improve ties', *New Straits Times*, 18 July 2001, p. 4. On 6 August 2001, a letter to the *New Straits Times* referred to the existence of the three preconditions, describing these as an example of US bullying. See M. Muhammad, 'US in no position to preach to others', p. 11.

[46] 'US Admonishes Malaysia', *FEER*, 2 August 2001, p. 8.

[47] 'Senate Foreign Relations Committee Hearing 25 July 2001', chaired by Senator John Kerry, 2 August 2001, www.freeanwar.com/facnews/senateforeigncommittee.

[48] And this despite the fact that the Heritage Foundation had been so outspoken in support of Anwar in 1998. Interviews conducted in Kuala Lumpur in February 2003 are important to this section.

[49] The caucus was inaugurated in April 2002 and was chaired by House Representative Pete

Sessions (Republican, Texas) and Representative Gregory Meeks (Democrat, New York), both of whom had visited Malaysia in January 2002 where they met with the prime minister and the governor of the Central Bank. *Bernama* (Malaysian National News Agency), 16 April 2002. Mahathir addressed the caucus's first meeting in Washington DC on 15 May 2002 and stressed that the US needed to be more tolerant of different cultures and values and called on it to be patient in demanding democracy because 'democracy could undermine the stability leading to war'. H. Kaur, 'Dr M: Make the world safe again', *New Straits Times*, 15 May 2002, p. 2. The caucus's fortunes have subsequently plummeted following a number of Mahathir's speeches critical of Bush administration foreign policy.

50 'U.S.–Malaysia Defense Cooperation: A Solid Success Story', Remarks by the Honorable Najib bin Tun Abdul Razak, Washington DC, 1 May 2002 (copy in the author's possession). See, too, 'Najib: Govt keeping close eye on discipline in Armed Forces', *Business Times*, 3 May 2002, p. 3.

51 'Remarks by the President and Prime Minister of Malaysia in Photo Opportunity', Oval Office, 14 May 2002, www.whitehouse.gov/news/releases/2002/; CNN.com reported that Mahathir had told reporters after the meeting that 'Bush had not raised the issues of human rights, democracy or the treatment of Anwar'. 'Malaysia, U.S. focus on terror fight', 15 May 2002.

52 D. E. Sanger, 'White House on Autocrats: Malaysian Si, Cuban No', www.nytimes.com/, 15 May 2002; interview with the Malaysian Prime Minister by Zain Verjee, www.CNN.com, 16 May 2002.

53 'Malaysiakini carries Powell's remarks on "flawed" trial of Anwar Ibrahim', *FBIS–East Asia*, 'Daily Report', 30 July 2002; 'Top U.S. official meets wife of Malaysia's jailed politician Anwar', *Associated Press*, 30 July 2002.

54 'Speech on US Foreign Policy since 9/11', by Ambassador Marie T. Huhtala, 29 August 2002, http://usembassymalaysia.org.my/; 'Malaysiakini carries US ambassador's remarks on bilateral ties with Malaysia', *FBIS–Near East*, 'Daily Report', 29 August 2002. During an interview in Washington, I asked whether the Malaysian government had incurred any costs for the treatment that it continued to meet out to Anwar. My interviewee in the US Department of State pointed out that Malaysia had been granted observer status only at the autumn meeting of the Community of Democracies (held in Seoul in November 2002), a fact that I later discovered seemed to irritate the foreign ministry in Kuala Lumpur, but had apparently gone unnoticed among other high-level government officials. Interviews in Washington DC (November 2002) and Kuala Lumpur (February 2003).

55 'US Interests and Policy Priorities in Southeast Asia', *op. cit.*

56 'US Understands Reason for ISA, says Rais', *Bernama*, 11 May 2002; 'Malaysia's Abdullah rules out abolition of Internal Security Act', *FBIS–East Asia*, 'Daily Report', 16 June 2002. According to the deputy prime minister, 'other countries like the United States shared Malaysia's view that the ISA was a preventive law that should be used in certain situations without having to wait until the outbreak of something bad with security implications'.

57 For example, Mahathir called the

US decision to go to war the action of a 'cowardly and imperialist bully'. 'Malaysian PM Condemns Iraq War', *BBC News-World*, Asia-Pacific, 24 March 2003, http://newsvote.bbc.co.uk. In Davos, Switzerland, in January 2003, he stated: 'Sanity has deserted both sides. Just as, in the stone age, the man with the biggest club ruled, in our modern and sophisticated global village the country with the biggest killing power rules'. '"World War has Begun": Malaysia's Mahathir Assails US at Davos Opening', 24 January 2003, www.commondreams.org/ headlines03.

Chapter 5

[1] For a fuller discussion of the US–China relationship in the Bush era, see my article entitled 'Bush, China and Human Rights', *Survival*, vol. 45, no. 2, summer 2003, pp. 167-186.

[2] In October 2002, Attorney General John Ashcroft finalised this arrangement in Beijing and introduced the new appointee, Tony Lau, a member of the FBI for more than 20 years. See www.usembassy-china.org.cn/press/release/2002.

[3] 'US-China Cooperative Relationship is Growing Fast, Powell Says', 5 November 2003, http://usinfo.state.gov/

[4] Secretary of State Colin L. Powell, 'Remarks at Asia Society Annual Dinner', 10 June 2002, www.asiasociety.org.

[5] Nixon, as quoted in D.M. Lampton, 'Small Mercies: China and America after 9/11', *The National Interest*, no. 66, winter 2001/02, p. 107.

[6] J. Carter, *Keeping Faith: Memoirs of a President*, (London: Collins, 1982), pp. 207–209.

[7] L. Dittmer, 'Chinese Human Rights and American Foreign Policy: A Realist Approach', *The Review of Politics*, 63/3, 2001, pp. 421–459.

[8] See D.M. Lampton, 'America's China Policy in the Age of the Finance Minister: Clinton Ends Linkage', *China Quarterly*, no. 139, September 1994, pp.597-621.

[9] China ratified this treaty in February 2001, lodging a reservation to Article 8, which concerns the right of everyone to form and join a free trade union.

[10] Its first annual report appeared in October 2002.

[11] Professor Paul Gewirtz was appointed in 1997 as special adviser to Clinton on rule-of-law questions. The programme – funded by the Luce and Ford Foundations – had six main elements to it, including commercial and administrative law reform in China, the training of Chinese judges and lawyers, and establishing a legal information system. Rule-of-law programmes in the George W. Bush era receive congressional funding. As noted earlier, restrictions on military and some technology sales to China remain in place, although not solely for human-rights-related reasons.

[12] J.W. Garver, 'Sino-American relations in 2001: the difficult accommodation of two great powers', *International Journal*, 57/2, spring 2002, p. 287.

[13] R. Hutcheson, 'Speaking to Chinese Diplomat, Bush Criticizes China's Human Rights Record', *Knight Ridder/Tribune Business News*, 23 March 2001.

[14] The US has been a sponsor or co-sponsor of these resolutions most years since 1990. China always introduces a procedural 'no-action' resolution, which, apart from in 1995, it has won.

[15] Ambassador Shirin Tahir-Kheli, 'Remarks to the 57th Session of the UN Commission on Human Rights', 18 April 2001,

www.state.gov/g/drl/rls/rm/
2001/

16 J.W. Garver, 'Sino-American
relations in 2001: the difficult
accommodation of two great
powers', *op. cit.*, pp. 287–288.

17 K.H. Conger, and J.C. Green,
'Spreading Out and Digging in:
Christian Conservatives and State
Republican Parties', *Campaigns
and Elections*, 23/1, February 2002.

18 *Pattern of Global Terrorism – 2002*,
(Washington DC: Office of the
Coordinator for
Counterterrorism, Department of
State, April 2003), p. 16.

19 As Wang Lequan, the Communist
Party head in Xinjiang put it in
March 2002, the 'anti-terrorism
campaign has to a great extent
been beneficial to our crackdown
on terrorist forces. It has greatly
suppressed the space they have to
carry out their activities'. *FBIS-
China*, 'Daily Report', 6 March
2002.

20 '"East Turkestan" Terrorist Forces
Cannot Get Away With
Impunity', Information Office of
the State Council, Beijing,
21 January 2002.

21 D. Gladney, 'Xinjiang: China's
Future West Bank?' *Current
History*, September 2002, p. 269.

22 'China: Tibetan Executed, Others
Await Trial', Human Rights Watch
news, 28 January 2003. China
denied a US request to let an
observer attend the trial. The UN
High Commissioner for Human
Rights also wrote to the Chinese
authorities expressing his concern.

23 One notable absentee from the
approach seems to be Attorney
General John Ashcroft. During his
visit to China to introduce the
new FBI attaché, he was asked
whether he had brought up
human-rights issues in his
discussions. He dissembled in his
reply. See www.usembassy-
china.org.cn/press/release/2002/,
24 October 2002.

24 W. Lam, 'Widening the Definition

of Terrorism' *China Brief*, vol. 1,
issue 8, 25 October 2001.

25 *FBIS–China*, 'Daily Report',
22 February 2002.

26 *FBIS–China*, 'Daily Report', 25
November 2002. Clark Randt also
stated that, if China wanted 'to be
accepted as both a respected and
responsible member of the
international community', then its
behaviour in this issue area had
to improve. The meeting itself
resulted in the release of Xu
Wenli, the founder of the China
Democracy Party, and apparent
agreement that China would
invite the UN special rapporteurs
on torture, arbitrary detention
and religious freedom to visit the
country without preconditions. R.
J. Saiget, 'China to invite UN
human rights experts
immediately, US says', *Agence
France Press*,17 December 2002.

27 See the press statement by the US
embassy in Beijing, *FBIS-China*,
29 August 2002.

28 During interviews conducted in
Washington DC in November
2002, all US officials stressed that
the timing was unfortunate,
unconnected with these missile-
control regulations, and entirely
explained by the gathering of
new intelligence data on this
small organisation.

29 US Department of State, Daily
Press Briefing, 22 March 2002,
www.state.gov/r/pa/prs/dpb/
2002.

30 *Patterns of Global Terrorism – 2001*,
op. cit.

31 *FBIS–Sov*, 'Daily Report', 30 June
2002, and *FBIS–China*, 'Daily
Report', 29 August 2002

32 D. Murphy, and S. V. Lawrence,
'Beijing hopes to gain from US
raids on Afghanistan', *FEER*,
4 October 2001, p. 20.

33 See, for example, D. C. Gladney,
'China's Minorities: the case of
Xinjiang and the Uyghur People',
paper for the UN Sub-
Commission on Promotion and

Protection of Human Rights, UN Documents, E/CN.4/Sub.2/ AC.5/2003/WP.16, 5 May 2003.

[34] Thus, when the US embassy released a statement in August 2002 echoing the Chinese claim that the ETIM was responsible for more than 200 acts of terrorism in China, the US press and the NGOs immediately demanded proof and criticised it for its inaccuracies and simplistic tone. *FBIS-China*, 'Daily Report', 29 August 2002.

[35] Admittedly, many Uighur groupings are distressed at this designation of the ETIM as terrorist, arguing that it has seriously sullied the broader almost entirely peaceful struggle against Chinese oppression, and given the Chinese further opportunities to oppress Uighurs in Xinjiang. Some did take comfort from Craner's speech in Xinjiang, however, stating that his 'trip to the region has given the Uyghurs a lot of hope that Washington hasn't abandoned them and dispelled the suspicious feeling some felt after U.S. put ETIM on the terrorist list'. Uyghur Information Agency, press release, 22 December 2002.

[36] *Ibid*.

[37] 'U.S. Not to Sponsor China Resolution at Rights Talks',

11 April 2003, www.nytimes.com/reuters/politi cs/; 'Dalai Lama: Envoy will visit Beijing', *Associated Press*, 7 April 2003; 'Four Tibetan detainees released in China, rights group says', *Associated Press*, 10 April 2003.

[38] Ming Wan's point in *Human Rights in Chinese Foreign Relations: Defining and Defending National Interests*, (Philadelphia: University of Pennsylvania Press, 2001).

[39] This approach is discussed in P. Pan, 'Prisoner Lists Now an Aid to U.S.-China Ties', *The Washington Post*, 18 October 2002, p. A20.

[40] Strongly argued in 'China and the Future of US-China Relations', Remarks to the National Committee on US-China Relations, by Richard N. Haass, Director, Policy Planning Staff, 5 December 2002. As regards the US message on the sharing of values, however, Chinese publications have frequently reported the human rights abuses by US agencies and officials that have occurred after 11 September.

Conclusion

[1] See http://news.bbc.co.uk/1/hi/ world/asia-pacific/, 18 April 2003.